More praise for *Library: An Unquiet History*

"Engrossingly saturated with fascinating lore, colorful anecdotes and deft portraits . . . [*Library*] entertainingly traces the evolution of the library through the centuries, from 'temple to market, from canon to cornucopia.' "   —*New York Times Book Review*

"A splendidly articulate, informative and provoking piece of work. . . . [*Library*] is sweeping in its inclusiveness, extraordinarily brisk in narrative vigor, and consistently lively . . . a book among books, to be savored and gone back to."   —*Baltimore Sun*

"Stimulating . . . the Dewey system lacks a category unique enough to place Battles's quirky labors."   —*Boston Sunday Globe*

"The transmission of knowledge from generation to generation is one of the miracles of civilization, with the crucial role libraries play in the process frequently ignored. Matthew Battles knows his way around the stacks as well as anyone; as a gifted and eloquent writer, he brings insight and humanity to their story. This book is a delight."
—Nicholas A. Basbanes,
author of *A Gentle Madness* and *Patience & Fortitude*

"Matthew Battles' discursive inquiry into the life and death of libraries has acquired horrific relevance . . . for all its contemporary resonances, *Library* is an old-fashioned work, idiosyncratically pursuing the author's interests through sentences and paragraphs notable for their elegant prose and arresting insights. . . . This is not a book for scholars, but for general readers, most of whom will be charmed by Battles' engaging voice and human portrait of libraries. . . . Battles' sprightly narrative performs a valuable service by blowing the dust off our stodgy, conventional conception of the library to reveal the living heart of cultures that beats beneath its stone facade."   —*Los Angeles Times Book Review*

"This is an idiosyncratic and brave book. . . . Innate to the human condition is a desire for knowledge, and Mr. Battles requires of his readers only that they be willing to decide the questions themselves based on the information he presents to them. As a result, his book, like many other fine works of literature, is not unlike a library."

—*Dallas Morning News*

"[A] remarkable volume for the stacks. . . . Battles' book is an obvious choice for bibliophiles. But the author's evident enthusiasm for his subject just might fan into flame any passion for books and libraries that smolders in the heart of the general reader, too."   —*Boston Herald*

"Informative, succinct and invigorating. . . . Battles eruditely traces the enormous importance of libraries to the evolution of civilization. . . . An informative, nourishing read."   —*Seattle Times/Post Intelligencer*

"One might expect a book that deals with three millennia's worth of what some might consider arcane history to be huge in scope and academically dry in presentation. *Library* is neither.. . . . [An] engaging book."   —*BookPage*

"The charm of Battles' book lies in its historical sweep and its appreciation for the browser's delight. . . . We need thoughtful critics like Battles not just to chronicle the library's institutional past but to defend its future."   —*Newsday*

"Highly readable and thoughtful."   —*Toronto Star*

"A must for every home or institutional collection." —*Kirkus Reviews*

"Elegantly written. . . . A great read, flowing over many time periods and geographic regions, from the great library at Alexandria to the war-ravaged libraries of Bosnia."   —*Library Journal*

"Battles writes in an engaging way and his book will be appreciated by librarians and book lovers."   —*Booklist*

"*Library* [is] a treasure. . . . It is nothing short of panoramic, using the broad scope of a history of civilization to illuminate the details of one of its most specific accomplishments: the book. . . . Despite the overwhelming task undertaken here, the author stays on track. . . . Come into this book with your own passions and the stories will meet your terms. They are rich in detail, academically minded, and yet full of popular appeal."   —*Elliot Bay Booknotes*

"Battles skillfully weaves the history of the library . . . a valuable addition to the history of the intellectual process, and a pretty good read to boot. Battles presents the course of history over the millennia with a deft hand and an eye for illuminating anecdotes that help to bring the vast sweep of history to life. . . . *Library* will make a valuable addition to your bookshelf, and people will be able to tell a lot about you if they find it there."   —*State*, Columbia, South Carolina

"If you ever thought that libraries were dull, Matthew Battles will change your mind."   —*The National Post*, Toronto

"There certainly isn't anything quiet in [Battles'] retelling of the destruction of millions of books by the Nazis or the siege of the Bosnian National and University Library. But for each act of destruction, Battles highlights the building of outstanding collections and zeroes in on the unique role of libraries in society."   —*American Libraries*

"There is not one [book about books] that is more informative, succinct and invigorating than this work by Battles. . . . It's a nourishing read for anyone interested in the history of books and their upkeep."
—*State Journal*, Lansing, Michigan

"[A] comprehensive literary tour . . . [taking] readers not on a survey of the buildings themselves but the literature they contain . . . delightful for its historical perspective, eclectic abundance of literary and library lore . . . [this] history of learning lost and found reminds us that we cannot erase our past by burning the library or improve our future by repeating the errors of our past."   —*The Advocate*

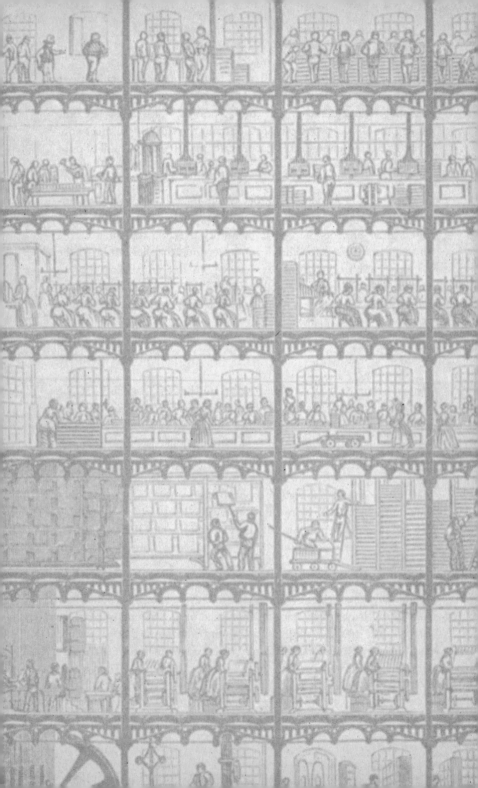

Library

AN UNQUIET HISTORY

Matthew Battles

W. W. NORTON & COMPANY

NEW YORK ✦ LONDON

FOR MY FAMILY
and
FOR KEN CARPENTER
Keeper of books

Copyright © 2003 by Matthew Battles

For information about permission to reproduce selections from this book, write to
Permissions, W. W. Norton & Company, Inc., 500 Fifth Avenue, New York, NY 10110

Manufacturing by Quebecor World, Fairfield Inc.
Book design by BTD
Production manager: Andrew Marasia

LIBRARY OF CONGRESS CATALOGING-IN-PUBLICATION DATA

Battles, Matthew.
Library : an unquiet history / by Matthew Battles.— 1st ed.
p. cm.
Includes bibliographical references and index.
ISBN 0-393-02029-0
1. Libraries—History. 2. Libraries and society—History. 3. Books—History. I. Title.
Z721.B28 2003
027'.009—dc21

2002156439

ISBN 0-393-32564-4 pbk.

W. W. Norton & Company, Inc., 500 Fifth Avenue, New York, N.Y. 10110
www.wwnorton.com

W. W. Norton & Company Ltd., Castle House, 75/76 Wells Street, London W1T 3QT

2 3 4 5 6 7 8 9 0

Contents

Acknowledgments

My gratitude tells the story of the writing of this book: I am indebted first to Donovan Hohn, gifted writer, genius editor, and good friend, who during his time at *Harper's* managed to cobble a serviceable magazine article from the hundred or so rambling emails I sent him; I am grateful for his perseverance, his taste, and his good faith. Passages from that article ("Lost in the Stacks: The Decline and Fall of the Universal Library," *Harper's Magazine*, January 2000), in much different form, are scattered throughout this book. Parts of chapter 2 appeared in my article "Burning Isn't the Only Way to Lose a Book," a review of *The Library of Alexandria: Centre of Learning in the Ancient World* (cited elsewhere), which appeared in the April 13, 2000, issue of the *London Review of Books*. I delivered a portion of chapter 2 as part of a talk for the History of Libraries in the United States conference at the Library Company of Philadelphia in April 2002. Susan Barry, my agent, persuaded me that the aforementioned ramblings about the life of libraries might make the beginnings of a book. She also helped me find my way to W. W. Norton and editor Alane Salierno Mason, without whose guidance and judgment this book would have gone off course at any number of points in its writing. Otto Sonntag, my copy editor at Norton, faced the task of bringing my untamed manuscript to heel; his efforts strengthened the book immeasurably. I'm also indebted to Ravi Mirchandani, my editor at

Heinemann in Britain, who offered his support, as well as his genius for titles, long before we began work on the U.K. edition. Thanks, too, to Nancy Fish of the Harvard Bookstore for sharing her wisdom on title troubles. In Rome, I was grateful for the opportunity to lodge at the American Academy, where I benefited as much from the remarkable company of the fellows there as from the Academy's happy proximity to the Vatican. Massimo Ceresa, the Vatican Library's reference librarian, provided both wisdom and hospitality, and his students at the library school at the Vatican were generous with their time and views on the world of the library in Europe. In London, my wife's cousin Althea Greenan, her companion Gavin, and their daughters played host to me and my family for a delightful week in their East Dulwich flat. Good friends and great writers James Parker and Joshua Glenn read numerous early drafts; their patience and insight was crucial to me. I owe a great debt of gratitude to all my colleagues and friends at Harvard, without whose indefatigable diligence that university's libraries would not thrive as they do. Those librarians and staff have been the true faculty of my own private postgraduate course in library studies. I'm particularly indebted to Peter Accardo, Anna Arthur, and Marek Kornilowicz for their friendship and insights; to András Riedlmayer for his patient and generous intelligence; to Librarian of Houghton Library William P. Stoneman; and especially to Kenneth Carpenter, a librarian and scholar of great and generous sagacity, who mentored me in my first two years of library work and whose guidance continues to brighten my professional life. My greatest thanks, of course, goes to my family, both by birth and by marriage, whose support and love are a constant revelation. And especially I thank my wife, Rebekah Schlesinger, who let me mumble her off to sleep with numerous drafts, and who as I write these words is outside allowing herself to be soaked with waterguns, drawing fire and giving cover, once again, to my writing.

Library

CHAPTER ONE

Reading the Library

The impious maintain that nonsense is normal in the Library and that the reasonable (or even humble and pure coherence) is a miraculous exception.

— JORGE LUIS BORGES, "The Library of Babel"

When I first went to work in Harvard's Widener Library, I immediately made my first mistake: I tried to read the books. I quickly came to know the compulsive vertigo that Thomas Wolfe's Eugene Gant, prowling the fictionalized Widener stacks, felt in the novel *Of Time and the River*:

Now he would prowl the stacks of the library at night, pulling books out of a thousand shelves and reading them like a madman. The thought of these vast stacks of books would drive him mad: the more he read, the less he seemed to know—the greater the number of the books he read, the greater the immense uncountable number of those which he could never read would seem to be. . . . He read insanely, by the hundreds, the thousands, the ten thousands. . . . [T]he thought that other books were waiting for

him tore at his heart forever. He pictured himself as tearing the
entrails from a book as from a fowl.

Gant's histrionics are a response to the contradictions anyone faces
in the library. As the reader gropes the stacks—lifting books and test-
ing their heft, appraising the fall of letterforms on the title page,
scrutinizing marks left by other readers—the more elusive knowledge itself becomes. All that remains unknown seems to beckon
from among the covers, between the lines. In the library, the reader
is wakened from the dream of communion with a single book, star-
tled into a recognition of the word's materiality by the sheer number of bound volumes; by the sound of pages turning, covers
rubbing; by the rank smell of books gathered together in vast numbers. Of course, the experience of the physicality of the book is
strongest in the large libraries, where the accumulated weight of
written words seems to exert a gravity all its own. And fewer
libraries are larger than Widener, which beguiled not only Thomas
Wolfe but myself and countless others as well.

Endowed by the grieving mother of Harry Elkins Widener, a
Harvard graduate and bibliophile who went down with the *Titanic*,
Widener is the Great Unsinkable Library. Its ten levels contain fifty-
seven miles of shelves, enough to hold some 4.6 million bound volumes, give or take a few. The shelves are great armatures of forged
iron that carry the weight of the building; the library quite literally is
supported by its books. Peopled not only with librarians, patrons, and
professors but also with carpenters, couriers, cooks, accountants, student and part-time book shelvers, webmasters, network administrators, and human resource consultants, it is the city-state at the center
of a confederacy of Harvard's ninety-odd school and departmental
collections, totaling some 14 million volumes; taken together, they
make up the largest academic library the world has ever known.

Among Widener's dusty stacks are tunnels: one leads to the government document depository, in which I have read Indian censuses recording how many houses are made of mud and grass, or how many basket weavers and hide tanners reside in each village in Uttar Pradesh or Kashmir. Another tunnel leads to the stacks that hold the theater collection and the "X-cage," which hides items in odd sizes and formats, on paper deemed too fragile for the open stacks, or of a nature too salacious for the eyes of the undergraduates of various eras. Here, piles of slim boxes contain philological notes written in a flowing, nineteenth-century hand; binders are stuffed thick with typescripts in Georgian and photostats of Averroës manuscripts. There are crumbling volumes of anti-immigrant tracts and pro-Nazi American magazines—sequestered not for the ideas they contain, but because the acid in their depression-era paper is causing the pages slowly to digest themselves. In this locked-away, seldom visited corner of the library, I come across the title *Military German: A "Lingo" Language Game*. It consists of a box of cards the size of a pack of unfiltered cigarettes with a booklet of instructions. "Questioning prisoners of war on the European front demands a specialized vocabulary," it says. "You learn it by playing cards and having fun at it!" The cards contain such useful phrases as "This is no time for arguments. Get out" *(Das ist keine Zeit zum Streiten! Raus!)* and "In spite of your lies I intend to give you another chance" *(Trotz Ihrer Lügen, beabsichtige ich, Ihnen noch eine Gelegenheit zu geben)*. A companion title treating Japanese states, "Most language manuals are for tourists. Not this one. This one is for American soldiers and sailors engaged in licking hell out of the Japs."

But the library—especially one so vast—is no mere cabinet of curiosities; it's a world, complete and uncompletable, and it is filled with secrets. Like a world, it has its changes and its seasons, which belie the permanence that ordered ranks of books imply. Tugged by the gravity of readers' desires, books flow in and out of the library like the tides. The people who shelve the books in Widener talk about the library's *breathing*—at the start of the term, the stacks exhale books in great swirling clouds; at end of term, the library inhales, and the books fly back. So the library is a body, too, the pages of books pressed together like organs in the darkness.

In the Widener stacks more than anywhere else, I can fool myself that the universe is composed of infinite variations of a single element—the book—that I, too, am made of books, like the person in Giuseppe Arcimboldo's painting *The Librarian*. The Prague court of Arcimboldo's patron, Rudolf II, freely mixed the rational and the irrational, the mythological and the empirical; Tycho Brahe and Johannes Kepler mingled with alchemists and astrologers. Arcimboldo reveled in the contradictions that surrounded him. This revel—and revelation—is embodied in his *Librarian*, a person made of books; he is not a single book but a whole library. His cheeks and lips are miniature books, the sort that in Arcimboldo's time would have contained prayers and devotions. His right arm, by contrast, is a weighty folio volume. Pages fan out from his head, marked not with type but with handwriting, legible only from above.

In the stacks of the library (this or any other), I have the distinct impression that its millions of volumes may indeed contain the entirety of human experience: that they make not a model *for* but a model *of* the universe. Fluttering down the foot-worn marble stairs that drop into the building's bowels, descending through layer after layer of pungent books, I am often struck by the sense that everything happening outside must have its printed counterpart somewhere in the stacks. It's easy to plunge into cabalistic reveries, dreaming rearrangements of the books that would reveal the mysteries of the universe, a sacred Logos tantamount to the secret name of God. Where among the 43 books published in Bhutan in

Giuseppe Arcimboldo, The Librarian, *ca. 1566. By permission of Skokloster Castle, Sweden, © LSH photo Goran Schmidt.*

1983, or the 31,602 published in China, or the 30,000 tablets at Ashurbanipal's long-lost library at Nineveh, or the 300,000 scrolls burned when Caesar flamed his ships at Alexandria, might we have sought the formula for the philosophers' stone? To which of the eight daily newspapers of Western Samoa should we look? Was the name of God carted off to the bookbinders in a ripped manuscript stolen from Salisbury Cathedral during the troubled reign of Henry VIII? Or encoded among some number of the 2,635 children's books published in Iran in 1996 alone? There's a reductive danger in this fantasy: for if the world can be compressed into a library, then why not into a single book—why not into a single word?

From the 1870s to the 1990s, the collections of research libraries at Harvard and elsewhere have increased a hundredfold—in some cases, a thousandfold. This vast torrent of books inspires in many people an awful shock and anxiety. All these books—who has time to read them? The apocryphal eighteenth-century *Old Librarian's Almanack* (actually a literary hoax perpetrated by a Boston librarian in the early twentieth century) extols the virtues of the librarian who diligently dusts his way through the books in his charge, taking the time to read each volume; when he reaches the last book, he begins the process again. The librarian in the research library of today could not accomplish this task in a lifetime—not in three hundred lifetimes. And of course, the collections aren't frozen. This library, like all research libraries of any size, acquires more books each year than any one of us could read in a lifetime. The Library of Congress, the world's largest universal library, each day adds some 7,000 books to the more than 100 million items already standing on its 530 miles of shelves. Add to this the printed ephemera we daily produce at our word processors, fax machines, and photocopiers, plus the more than 800 million pages on the World Wide Web, and it becomes clear: we are inundated.

This flood of print forces us to ask, How do we sort it all out? Until fairly recently—that is to say in the last couple of hundred years, which is a short interval for the library—librarians could have counted themselves among the Stoic followers of Seneca, who, in his *Epistulae morales*, wrote that "it does not matter how many books you have, but how good they are." Seneca's library is a place of canons. I like to call this type of library the "Parnassan," for like Delphi it is a temple built upon the flanks of Mount Parnassus, that hilltop holy to Apollo and the Muses. The works within it are a distillation, the essence of all that is Good and Beautiful (in the classical formulation) or Holy (in the medieval). It is meant as a model for the universe, a closely orchestrated collection of ideals. In the universal library, by contrast, books are not treated as precious and crystalline essences, at least not in the first instance. Instead, they are texts, fabrics to be shredded and woven together in new combinations and patterns. Like the stars in the sky or the flowers of Linnaeus, they are not to be praised for particular influences or qualities; they must be counted and classified before they may be desired.

Grumpy Seneca gave the selective Parnassan library a motto fit to inscribe in Roman capitals above the doors. Thomas Jefferson (whose own books were the kernel of the collections of the University of Virginia and the Library of Congress) offers the relentlessly accumulative universal library a contrasting creed: "a library book . . . is not, then, an article of mere consumption but fairly of capital." Each sort of library is also an argument about the nature of books, distilling their social, cultural, and mystical functions. And what the Word means to society—whether it is the breath of God or the Muses, the domicile of beauty and the good, the howling winds of commerce, or some ambiguous amalgam of all these things— this is what the library enshrines. Ultimately, there may be a common creed under which the Parnassan and the universal libraries—with their attendant conceptions of the book and the Word—can be united. If so, perhaps it is the one offered by Stéphane Mallarmé, who expressed best my own experience in the library when he wrote that "everything in the world exists to end up in a book."

In *Of Grammatology*, Jacques Derrida sets out to show that writing is no mere secondary system of symbols for the spoken word, a "trace of a trace," but is, in short, its own thing. He needn't have looked farther than the universal library for support. For here the written word takes on a life of its own in the jumble of incipits, explicits, and colophons; of pages recto and verso; of manuscript in hands uncial and Beneventan and Merovingian Compressed; in palimpsests and lacunae; in sewn signatures from folio to octavo to sexagesimo-quarto; in chain lines and watermarks, in incunabula and CD-ROMs; in the *Pandectarum* and the *Index Librorum Prohibitorum*; in subject, author, and title cards; and in the subfields and literals of the MARC record format.

Like other natural philosophers of the Latin Middle Ages, Roger Bacon held that three classes of substance were capable of magic: the herbal, the mineral, and the verbal. With their leaves of fiber, their inks of copperas and soot, and their words, books are an amalgam of the three. The notion that words, like plants and stones, have existences independent of our uttering them—that they have power and do things in the world—is a commonplace in many traditions. Brought together in multitudes, heaped up and pared down, read and forgotten, library books take on lives and histories of their own, not as texts but as physical objects in the world.

Let me give an example, one from the library in which I work. In 1503 in Savona, Italy, the printer Francesco de Silva produced the first edition of Domenico Nani Mirabelli's *Polyanthea opus suavissimis floribus exornatum*, a popular compendium and dictionary of classical authors. Like all books of the time, the *Polyanthea* would have been

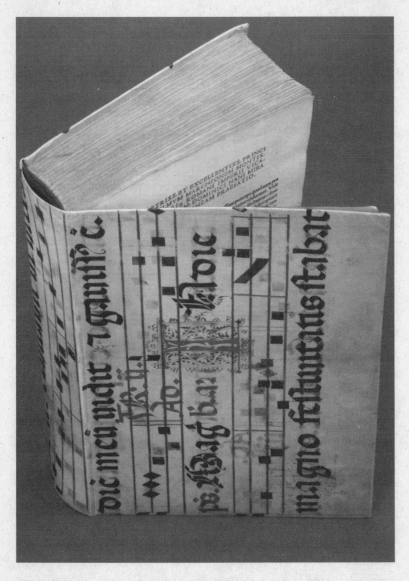

The Polyanthea of Nani Mirabelli (1503), a printed book bound in a leaf from a manuscript antiphonary. Houghton Library, Typ 525 03.596 F. By permission of the Department of Printing & Graphic Arts, Houghton Library, Harvard University. Photograph by Stephen Sylvester and Bob Zinck, HCL imaging services.

sold unbound, in loose signatures; individual buyers would bring the freshly printed pages to a binder, who would encase them in a covering as simple or ornate as the customer's taste—and pocketbook—permitted. Students might have left the sheaves unbound, sharing pages from a single volume with fellow students to cut down on expenses. A wealthy collector, by contrast, would have had the book clad in richly gilded leather, dyed to match the colors of his already extensive library. The copy in Houghton Library, however, was rebound sometime in the last five hundred years. The material for its binding was taken from another work altogether: a manuscript antiphonary of uncertain pre-Gutenberg provenance, in vellum, its three-line musical staves lined up precisely along the edges of the book, forcing manuscript and print, soaring music and marching text, into uneasy intimacy.

This practice was common among the early printers and binders. When King Henry VIII broke with the Roman Catholic Church, the abbeys' new, secular owners often swiftly emptied them of books, which they sold as pulp for use in preparing the papers and bindings of new volumes. A few Tudor luminaries saw this for the destruction it was: Richard Cotton, one of the king's own ministers, secretly saved many works from the bindery, including the earliest still-surviving copy of *Beowulf.* The same thing happened throughout Europe in the early decades of the print era: the only extant written example of the Old Saxon dialect, for example, was found stiffening the binding of a volume in the Vatican Library. Abandoned texts and ephemera—the lifeblood of the universal library—continued to be recycled in this fashion for centuries. Peer behind the flaky leather covering the spine of nearly any French book published up to the turn of the century, and you will find the bold capitals of advertising pages, torn into strips and pressed into service.

Even before the advent of movable type, when books were a

costly, specialized technology, manuscripts were recycled. Vellum could be scraped down to remove any writing it may have carried—a list of some obscure laird's serfs, or perhaps the earliest rendering of Cicero's denunciation of Catiline to the Senate—producing a clean page ready to receive fresh copy. Examples of such reused manuscripts are called palimpsests; the ghost of manuscript past remains, sometimes legible only in ultraviolet light, beneath the new generation of handwriting.

Many indices of the passage of time are inscribed into the physical matter of books. One finds dates of acquisition stamped or penciled onto the verso of title pages; charge slips record whether, when, and how often books have been taken out. In the condition of bindings and papers, time loses its linear nature, revealing its fluid, clotty relation to our experience. Recently published books often are worried to a state of utter decay—their boards battered, their spines loose, their pages ripped and scribbled upon. Some older books, by contrast, have never been peered into by even the most persistent patron: pages remain uncut, unsmudged. When they are finally plucked from the shelves, their bindings crack when opened, as tight as when they left the bindery. Charge slips have browned and crumbled away without seeing a single stamp. Card catalogs once displayed patterns of use of the collection over time, oft-consulted cards becoming more dog-eared and smudged as they were thumbed and held, while unconsulted cards remained fresh and white in their interiors, pressed and protected by their neighbors. The card catalogs are largely gone, of course; now online catalogs register visitors in the occult fashion of great digital networks. Not only do these systems record the borrowing of books; the computers track the number of times each record is viewed as well, chronicling the searches taking place on workstations throughout the network.

Some have pointed out the monstrosity of the online catalog, that grotesque tentacular database which has the capacity to turn even the coolest of scholar-patrons into a gibbering fool. They mourn the loss of the virtues of the card catalog, that elegant labor of generations of librarians. If we heed the warnings of librarians present at the invention of the card catalog itself, however, we might not so hastily make our retreat. Edmund Lester Pearson, writing in 1909, observed,

As these cabinets of drawers increase in number until it seems as if the old joke about the catalogues of the Boston Public Library and Harvard University meeting on Harvard Bridge might become literally true, the mental distress and physical exhaustion suffered by those consulting one of them becomes too important to be disregarded.

Almost any day in any large library their fearful influence may be observed. Dozens of harrowed individuals are seen trying to think whether the name of Thomas De Quincy will be found in the drawer marked De or that labelled Qu. Then they make the choice—always wrong—and are seen, with pain only too apparent on their brows, dashing off to the other drawer. . . .

Nor . . . are the consulters of the catalogues the only persons whose reasons are in danger. The cataloguers themselves, the very ones who sit all day spinning this codified brainstorm, are in peril. Not long ago a body of them got together and bound themselves by a fearful oath not to part until they had settled once and for-ever the question whether it is better to write "Department of Agriculture" or "Agriculture, Department of." They well knew that many a strong mind has come to ruin on this reef, but they were a reckless lot, and they plunged in. Midnight came, and found them still bickering. The struggle continued during the early hours of the morning, and at last the cold gray light of dawn looked in at the shutters, but whatever it saw, no solution of the problem was there, and the mental condition of the disputants has ever since been one upon which it is not pleasant to dwell.

And this was the case in that universal library circa 1900, with its collections a hundred times smaller than those of the research library of today. The anxieties of Pearson's patron and catalogers may have less to do with the size of libraries or the nature of their catalogs than with the metaphysical implications of the idea of the universal library itself.

Systems of classification record history at another, coarser level of detail. American academic libraries have adopted the now standard Library of Congress call number system—an opaque cabalism of numbers and letters defiant of intuition, replete with the formulaic rigor of "scientific" bibliography. There are other systems, too, of which Dewey's is probably the most (in)famous. Most libraries once had their own proprietary systems of call numbers as well. Widener's old system persists in the stacks to this day, preserving traces of the division of knowledge in its turn-of-the-century formulation. The "Aus" class contains books on the history of the Austro-Hungarian Empire; the "Ott" class serves the purpose for the Ottoman Empire. Dante, Molière, and Montaigne each gets a class of his own.

In the universal library, esoterica and exoterica mingle in disregard for the patterns and preferences of their respective times. One finds shelved side by side numerous editions of the Variorum Shakespeare; intershelved among them are such legitimately obscure works as *Shakespeare in Limerick,* by Brainerd McKee, a 1910 doggerel adaptation of the collected works of the Bard of Avon. Here is McKee'a abridgment of *The Tempest*, with that obsessive librarian Prospero nowhere to be found:

> There once was a girl named Miranda
> Who flirted with one Ferdinand, a
>   Shipwrecked young prince
>   Who, after a rinse,
> Played chess with her on the veranda.

Henry David Thoreau could have been reading such doggerel in the dim alcoves of Harvard's Gore Hall when he wrote, "[I]n a library [t]here is all the recorded wit of the world, but none of the recording, a mere accumulated, and not truly cumulative treasure; . . . Shakespeare and Milton did not foresee into what company they were to fall." Even for Thoreau—who browsed nature as if it were the most copious library of all, who found genius and grandeur expressed fully in its least significant details—bad books in the library fall like hail on literature's eternal spring morn. But the same sort of secret wonders Thoreau discovered among furtive squirrels and browsed-over apple trees is alive in the library, too. Must one choose from among the collection of numerological treatises which prove that it was Francis Bacon who wrote the Bard's plays, or the close chronological studies that restore the authorship of Edward de Vere, earl of Oxford, or the (many volumes fewer) biographical literature supporting the Stratfordian himself? No; these books must stand together on the shelves of any truly universal library. Together they tell us stories that they could not tell alone.

Reading the library, we quickly come to an obvious conclusion: most books are bad, very bad in fact. Worst of all, they're *normal*: they fail to rise above the contradictions and confusions of their times (in this respect, I'm sure this book will be no exception). It's understandable, then, that we spend so much energy ferreting out the exceptional books, the ones that shatter paradigms. But we shouldn't forget that the unremarkable books have much to teach us about cultural history—ultimately more, perhaps, than our cherished Great Books. In his *Atlas of the European Novel*, Franco Moretti argues that the "series"—the chronological context from which the exceptional works always spring—is "the true protagonist of cultural life." Moretti admits that "[a] history of literature as history of norms" may seem a "less innovative, much 'flatter' configuration than the one we are used to. . . . But this is exactly what life is like, and instead of redeeming literature from its prosaic features we should learn to recognize them and understand what they mean."

AS THE FULLNESS OF A CULTURE is expressed in its literature taken as a whole, so have the authors of books intuited the significance of the library. Libraries figure in the work of writers ranging from Shakespeare to Jonathan Swift to Umberto Eco. Indeed, the library is such an evocative setting that it has become a cliché; what would a gothic mystery be without a gloomy library? (Noticing the great lateral strength of books—just smack your palm with the spine of even the flimsiest paperback, and you'll see what I mean—I've had a notion of writing a murder mystery in which a book was the weapon. It always seemed to me the greatest loss of the game Clue that one could never do it to Colonel Mustard, in the library, with the *book*.) Libraries are so enticing to authors that they can't help making them up for themselves. Perhaps the first instance of this subgenre is found in the second book of Rabelais's *Gargantua and Pantagruel*, in which Pantagruel visits the library of Saint Victor's in Paris, browsing such choice titles as *The Codpiece of the Law* and *De modo cacendi* (On methods of shitting). For all his imaginative abundance, however, Rabelais did not exhaust the form:

John Donne penned a fictional bibliography in 1610; Edgar Allan Poe peppered his stories with citations from a library that existed only in his head; and Charles Dickens had the doors to the study in his house at Gad's Hill tricked out with false bookshelves containing such titles as *Hansard's Guide to Refreshing Sheep* (in nineteen volumes).

Perhaps the most famous literary library was imagined by an author who was also a librarian. In his short story "The Library of Babel," Jorge Luis Borges imagines the universe as a library (or perhaps it's the library he imagines as a universe). It's a curiously uniform library, however, a Platonic ideal, which according to the narrator is "composed of an indefinite and perhaps infinite number of hexagonal galleries." Four walls contain five bookshelves each; the two remaining walls open on adjacent, identical rooms. "Also through here," the narrator explains, "passes a spiral stairway, which sinks abysmally and soars upward to remote distances." In the halls are mirrors, which the narrator presumes "represent and promise the infinite" extent of the library. The experience of Babel's traveling librarians confirms that this pattern repeats itself indefinitely in all directions. The books that fill this library must be finite in extent— 410 pages each, their variation is limited by the fixed number of letters in the alphabet. Yet the librarians who populate this universe cannot conceive of a limit or border; the universe, they reason, must somehow be infinite.

For any question, the library offers no hope of a definitive answer: though it necessarily contains prophecies of the lives of everyone who has lived or will live, as well as theories explaining the origins and workings of the universe itself, it must also contain unimaginable numbers of spurious accounts, with no means of sorting the true and immanent from the fallacious and misleading. Librarians wander in tribes or as lonely mendicants; some search out the one book that catalogs all the rest; others seek "clarification of humanity's basic mysteries; still others believe that the books are meaningless," the work of vain primordial beings imitating the perfect architecture of the deity. But Borges's narrator believes he has discovered the cosmological key to the library, its final theory of everything: "*the library*," he writes, "*is unlimited and cyclical. If an eternal traveler were to cross it in any direction, after centuries he would see that the same volumes were repeated in the same disorder (which, thus repeated, would be an order: the Order).*"

Borges the librarian suffered from hereditary blindness, the fog of which ultimately stole from him visual delight in the physicality of books. His blindness became total about the same time that he was elevated to the directorship of Argentina's National Library after the fall of the Peronist regime.

> No one should read self-pity or reproach
> Into this statement of the majesty
> Of God, who with such splendid irony
> Granted me books and blindness in one touch.

Borges's loss of sight reminds me of Lavinia in Shakespeare's *Titus Andronicus*, whose own injuries also prevented her from reading. The sons of Tamora had raped her and, chopping off her hands and cutting out her tongue, had stolen her senses of touch and taste as well. Lavinia's agony is moving despite Shakespeare's reliance on a violence that is lurid in its irreality (further weakening a play so shaky that apologists long tried, without success, to attribute it to another author). She misses the taste of words; she cannot tell the story that would bring vengeance to her tormentors, and her agony reveals itself in her silence. When she enters Titus's library, he sees the grief in her eyes and bids a boy to turn the pages of whatever books she chooses. "Take choice of all my library," he tells her, "and so beguile thy sorrow." We are meant here to identify deeply with Lavinia's estrangement from intimacy with books, and our empathy should enliven our pity. But to Lavinia, it's not the beguiling solace of books that she craves but their ability to tell stories. And so she chooses Ovid's *Metamorphoses*, and with the stumps of her arms she tosses the pages to the story of Philomel. Remembering Philomel's rape at the hands of Tereus, Titus sees her point, and the wheels of justice begin to turn.

Borges, like Lavinia, was cut off from the sensuous experience of books. And yet the books were in him still; he was as much a library as that composite librarian in Arcimboldo's painting. In "Poem of the Gifts," Borges later states that to his occluded eyes the books of the library are now "as distant as the inaccessible volumes / that perished once in Alexandria."

Like one of Borges's lost librarians, I explore the library's intertwined relations of fancy and authenticity, of folly and epiphany, of the Parnassan and the universal. My method in the pages that follow mirrors that of Eugene Gant: I pick up a volume—perhaps it's Gibbon's *Decline and Fall*—and something I read there leads to the lyrics of Callimachus or the letters of Seneca. Keeping a finger stuck among those pages, I follow a trail that leads from Cassiodorus to Francis Bacon, from Caliph Omar to Jonathan Swift and John Stuart Mill. I drop one passage to follow another, threading my way among ranges of books, lost among the shelves. In many places, the volumes are thick with dust, pocked with the holes left by insects, which are almost as hungry for books as I.

For all this free association, however, my searching has a plan. I am looking for the library where it lives. Of course, a complete history of the library—a documentary account of libraries wherever they have existed, in whatever forms they take—would run to many volumes. What I'm looking for are points of transformation, those moments where readers, authors, and librarians question the meaning of the library itself. As I follow Borges, the blind librarian, out of the stacks and into the whirling data streams of the Internet, I experience less shock than I might have expected. Out there the searching is as casual, as associative, and as serendipitous as ever it was.

CHAPTER TWO

Burning Alexandria

To John the Grammarian, a Coptic priest living in Alexandria at the time of the Arab conquest in A.D. 641, the Muslim conqueror Amr must have seemed something of a novelty. When John was named adviser to the general, he was delighted to discover that the city's new governor was not so bored with music, poetry, and learning as barbarians are supposed to be. Soon John grew bold (and hopeful) enough to ask Amr what might be done with the "books of wisdom" held in the "royal treasuries"—the famous library contained in the palace of the Ptolemies. No doubt, he hoped the general would entrust the library to his hands. The general replied, however, that he could not decide the fate of the books without consulting Caliph Omar. The caliph's answer, quoted here from Alfred J. Butler's *Arab Conquest of Egypt*, is infamous: "Touching the books you mention, if what is written in them agrees with the Book of God, they are not required; if it disagrees,

they are not desired. Destroy them therefore." According to tradition, the scrolls were bundled up and delivered as fuel to the city's
baths, where it is said they fueled the furnaces for six months.

It's too bad that such a colorful tale, fit as it is for the *Thousand
and One Nights*, carries only the rudiments of truth. In fact, the story
as we know it may have been invented by one Ibn al-Qifti, a
twelfth-century Sunni chronicler. According to the Egyptian classicist Mostafa el-Abbadi, al-Qifti may have invented the story to jus-
tify the sale of books by the twelfth-century Sunni ruler Saladin,
who sold off whole libraries to pay for his fight against the Crusaders. Despite its possible Islamic origin, however, the story has
been handed down in the West as an Orientalist lament for the fate
of Hellenic learning in the heathen East.

In fact, by the time the caliph's army arrived at Alexandria in the
seventh century A.D., the city's storied library had seen at least one
major fire already, and perhaps more. There had been not only one
library but two: a great library founded in the third century B.C.
within the Mouseion, or temple of the Muses, and a smaller "daughter" library. Built in the following century, the latter was placed in the
temple of Serapis, a Hellenized Egyptian deity and divine patron of
syncretistic Alexandria, whom the theologically resourceful
Ptolemies had conjured for themselves. Both collections were housed
in the royal precinct, the Brucheion, and are often spoken of as a single entity. Outside the royal quarter, books would have been found
throughout the city in great quantities: home of the papyrus industry, Alexandria was the center of the book trade throughout the
Mediterranean almost from its founding to the third century A.D.

When Julius Caesar came to the aid of Cleopatra in her war
against young Ptolemy XIII in 48 B.C. (by which time the libraries
were already nearly three hundred years old), he burned the ships in
Alexandria's harbor to prevent his enemy from taking the city by

sea. According to Seneca, some forty thousand books were lost in the ensuing conflagration, though other authorities hold that only a few books, stored in the warehouses awaiting shelving, were burned. These books, in fact, were probably waiting for shipment to Rome on Caesar's orders. Even if Seneca's estimate is correct, it is dwarfed by the seven hundred thousand scrolls thought to have been in the main library of the Mouseion alone. There are rumors of subsequent fires, too; but visitors to Alexandria in the period following Caesar's death leave evidence of great libraries' continued existence. Strabo, who wrote in the time of Augustus and the birth of Jesus, seems to have been acquainted with a working Alexandrian library. Legend holds that Marc Antony offered Cleopatra the books of Pergamum (Alexandria's great rival, located in what is now the Turkish province of Izmir) as compensation for the loss of her library, though Plutarch doubts the truth of this tale. Suetonius writes that Domitian, Roman emperor of the second century A.D., employed Alexandrian scholars to replace the texts of Augustus's Palatine Library after it was destroyed in a fire; this would seem to indicate the ongoing presence of an intellectual community at Alexandria, holding precious texts from which copies could be produced. It is likely that what remained of the libraries was destroyed utterly in the third century A.D., when the Brucheion was razed during the emperor Aurelian's war against the notorious Zenobia, queen of Palmyra. By this time, however, the libraries surely were in decline under Christians who, following their cultural triumph over pagans, Jews, and Neoplatonists, found the Hellenic riches of the libraries discomfiting. Their ire reached a fever pitch in the fourth century A.D.: Theophilus, patriarch of Alexandria, desired the site of the temple of Serapis for a church; he set loose a mob of Christians, who destroyed the pagan temple and, perhaps, the books of its library as well. Whatever the truth of the tale of the caliph's decree three hundred years later, it seems clear that the flimsy papyrus of Alexandria burned more than once.

UNLIKE ALEXANDRIA'S COLLECTION of papyrus scrolls, the first libraries could not burn at all, for they were filled with books written in clay. The literature of Mesopotamia goes back to the third millennium B.C., and ranges from poetry to prayer, from epistle to account book. The script in which it was written, called cuneiform, is named for the shape of its syllabic characters, which consist of clusters of small, wedge-shaped marks incised into clay tablets with a stylus. The clay would be left to dry or fired in a kiln; the resulting "books" are extremely durable, especially in the dry climate of the Fertile Crescent. These durable books of clay lent themselves to the library-building impulse; as early as the third millennium B.C., a temple at the town of Nippur, in what is now southeastern Iraq, included archive rooms filled with tablets.

Mesopotamian libraries reached their zenith nearly two thousand years later, in the reign of Ashurbanipal II, who ruled the Assyrian Empire in the seventh century B.C. He organized a great library at his capital, the already ancient city of Nineveh, which grew to include as many as 25,000 tablets. While his library served as an archive, Ashurbanipal's aspirations were universal, and he ordered the collection not only of omens, incantations, and hymns but of the ancient literatures of the several Mesopotamian languages—Assyrian, Sumerian, Akkadian, Ugaritic, and Aramaic, among others. The library seems to have been highly organized; works were tied together in their various tablets and marked with a label to identify their contents; a catalog also existed, recording the titles of works and the number of tablets that comprised them. Other archives and libraries throughout Mesopotamia show similarly high levels of organization; in some repositories, tablets were kept in labeled bas-

kets, their titles written along the edges of the clay for quick iden-
tification. Given the great antiquity of these writings, the number
that have survived is astonishing: some twenty thousand fragments
exist from Ashurbanipal's library alone, now kept in the British
Museum. Ashurbanipal's successors could not administer the far-
flung lands he had conquered; the power of his empire quickly
waned after his death, and Nineveh was gradually abandoned and
forgotten. Still more Mesopotamian libraries must lie buried in the
great tells, or mounds of ruined cities, that dot the landscape of the
Assyrian homeland, now Iraq; precision bombs may now be destroying libraries we don't even know exist.

Four hundred years after the library at Nineveh crumbled,
Alexander the Great shattered the Near East. In 331 B.C., when he
decided to celebrate his conquests by building a great city on Egypt's
Mediterranean shore, he is said to have traced the perimeter of the
future Alexandria with a trail of flour. According to one account, a
great flock of wading birds arose from the shores of nearby Lake
Mareotis to follow him on his circumambulation, gobbling up the
flour as he went. At first, the conqueror took this as an ill omen, until
an adviser pointed out the true meaning: that Alexandria would
prosper and offer endless sustenance and wealth to its inhabitants.
However Alexander chose and planned his city, its location was aus-
picious; it offered the best port on the Egyptian Mediterranean and
the only point of access to the breadbasket of the Delta and the
inland Nile. Alexander died before seeing his aspirations for the city
fulfilled; his former general Soter made the city the capital of the
Ptolemy dynasty after the young conqueror's death. It was Soter
who envisioned the library that would concentrate—and give his
heirs dominion over—the learning of the Hellenic world.

Like all Greek lyceums of the time, the libraries of Alexandria
took Aristotle's Peripatetic school as their immediate inspiration.

Aristotle had been Alexander's tutor, and the name of his school came to denominate the followers of his rationalist philosophy. Originally, however, the term *peripatos*, which means, literally, "walking around," referred to his teaching method. He took his pedagogy from Plato, whose own teacher, Socrates, had walked and taught everywhere—on the roads, in the homes of his wealthy young followers, or in the agora, or marketplace, of Athens. Even in the fully literate Greek world, their wholly oral method had become the norm.

Some ancient sources claim that Aristotle's own library was transported to Alexandria, where it became the seed collection from which the great library grew. The great Greek geographer Strabo, however, who seems to have known the library well, tells that Aristotle's books had been buried in a hole in Athens, to keep them from being claimed by the Attalid kings, the rulers of Athens, who wanted them for their library at Pergamum. Later the books—water-damaged, worm-eaten—were dug up and sold to the book collector Apellicon, who in trying to collate and amend the damaged scrolls introduced many inaccuracies. His library would be claimed by the Roman general Sulla, who took Athens from the forces of King Mithridates VI in 88 B.C. He had the library packed up and sent back to Rome, where the books were split up, copied incorrectly, and all but lost.

Despite its Aristotelian inspiration, however, the library departed from the Peripatetic model in striking fashion. Although it was meant to attract scholars and thinkers, no formal teaching program was adopted. This was one of its chief benefits to scholars; for then as now, intellectuals found teaching as much a burden as a calling. The royal pension freed scholars from having to advertise for pupils to walk around with, while the heaps of scrolls offered them inexhaustible opportunities for their work.

Strabo describes the scene confronting readers at Alexandria, where indoor book stacks were surrounded by a series of open, breezy colonnades or covered walkways, to the shade of which the scholars could repair for study and discussion. Such colonnades, perhaps evoking Plato's shady grove, became a standard element in ancient libraries, and even Roman libraries—which like modern ones had reading rooms with tables and chairs—featured them.

Of course, the scholars weren't reading books, not as we know them; the codex, or bound book, would not come into use until the Christian era in Rome. Alexandria's libraries, like all ancient repositories, were filled instead with scrolls of papyrus, a water reed native to the banks of the Nile. Compared with clay, papyrus is fragile and hard to preserve. It was plentiful, however, and could be transformed into a convenient medium for writing quickly and easily. When hammered flat, juices in the plant act as a sort of cement to bind and fix the fibers: the first papermakers learned to split open individual plant stems, lay them overlapping each other, and pound them into sheets of any given length. Once dry, the resulting sheets were then wrapped around a peg, called an *umbilicus*. No physical evidence remains of Alexandria's libraries, and archaeological evidence from other, later libraries is of doubtful value in reconstructing the shelving and access of scrolls in their stacks. Contemporary descriptions, however, allow a few conclusions: Scrolls in libraries had tags marked with the authors and titles of the work hanging from these *umbilici*. This was especially necessary because scrolls, unlike codices, don't stand up on shelves; instead, scrolls had to be heaped together into precarious piles. To remove one scroll, a reader or library assistant would have had to shift all the others on the shelf; as a result, only a kind of generalized order would have been possible to maintain.

The scholars of the Mouseion ate together in a dining hall and held their property in common, much as medieval scholars did in the early universities of Europe. By all accounts, the scholars enjoyed an extraordinary degree of academic freedom; the Ptolemies seem to have understood that they would produce the most useful work only if given free rein. This privilege apparently extended even to dealings with the royal house; when Ptolemy I Soter, impatient with his own slow progress in mathematics, asked Euclid for a shortcut, the geometer had the temerity to reply, "There is no royal road to Geometry." The perks of a posting at Alexandria didn't fail to raise the ire of excluded scholars; one Timon of Phlius wrote derisively of the "cloistered bookworms" fed and cared for in Alexandria's "chicken coop of the muses" (I like to think it was Timon's mixed metaphors that took him out of the running for an Alexandrian tenure). By bringing scholars to Alexandria and inviting them to live and work, at royal expense, among an enormous store of books, the Ptolemies made the library into a think tank under the control of the royal house. The strategic implications of a monopoly on knowledge—especially in medicine, engineering, and theology, all among Alexandria's strengths—were not lost on the Ptolemies. They ordered the confiscation of the books of visitors to the city, which were copied for the libraries (though sometimes the originals were kept, too), adorned with a tag that read "from the ships." In an effort to stop the growth of the libraries at Rhodes and Pergamum, both of which threatened Alexandria's preeminence, the city's rulers banned the export of papyrus. The move backfired, however, spurring the Pergamenes to invent parchment (*charta pergamenum*), which for its strength and reusability would prove to be the preferred writing medium in Europe for more than a thousand years.

Despite competition from Rhodes, Athens, Pergamum, and other centers of Hellenic culture, Alexandria's libraries thrived under the Ptolemies. The names of scholars who followed the seven hundred thousand scrolls to Alexandria echo down to the present day; Euclid, who was probably born in the dusty Egyptian village that existed at the site before Alexander founded his city, wrote his *Elements* there, and Archimedes passed through as a student before settling in his beloved Syracuse. Eratosthenes, Strabo, and Galen all relied on the riches of Alexandria. Legend has it that, at Ptolemy II's urging, seventy Jewish scholars convened in the library to translate the Torah into Greek; the Septuagint was the miraculous result. Alexandria was home as well to the most cosmopolitan and eclectic school of Greek lyric poetry, whose most famous exponent, Callimachus, also served as librarian at the Mouseion. His 120-volume critical bibliography, the *Pinakes*, or tables, cataloged the vast collection of Greek literature held in the library. His catalog shared the fate of its library: none of this work has survived.

In the first centuries A.D., the city would be the scene of great cultural struggles among pagans, Jews, Christians, and Neoplatonists; what we know today as the Judeo-Christian tradition has its origins in the eclecticism of Alexandria. But the libraries always had a grander mission than any of these: they sought to compile and contain the entire corpus of Greek literature, as well as the most significant works of many foreign languages. Thus was Alexandria's the first library with universal aspirations; with its community of scholars, it became a prototype of the university of the modern era.

The great pile of books at Alexandria defined a newly acquisitive approach to the value of knowledge. The goal was to hold everything, from the authoritative manuscripts of the *Iliad* and Hesiod's *Works and Days* to the most obscure lists of secondary and fallacious commentaries on Homer, to works incorrectly attributed to Homer, the works pointing out their misattribution, and the works refuting those works. In furthering this goal, the Ptolemies made good on the essentially Alexandrian intuition that knowledge is a resource, a commodity, a form of capital to be acquired and hoarded at the pleasure of the regime. The centralization and consolidation of libraries serves the convenience of scholars and princes alike. But great libraries are problematic in times of war, disaster, or decay, for their fate becomes the fate of the literatures they contain. Much of what comes down to us from antiquity survived because it was held in small private libraries tucked away in obscure backwaters of the ancient world, where it was more likely to escape the notice of zealots as well as princes.

Above all, it is this last point—the needs and tastes of private readers and collectors—that determines what survives. Before the flames, before theft and censorship, the fate of books is bound up in the constant shuffling and transformation of the word in all its uses. Though Alexandria's libraries were universal in scope, their librarians faced hard choices. Manuscript scrolls were costly and time-consuming to produce, and the scribes' precious labor could not often be lavished on minor texts. The chief role of an ancient library was the provision of exemplars from which readers would transcribe copies for their own use; naturally, only the major works were copied in any great quantity. The rest—the secondary, the extra-canonical, and the apocryphal—dropped out of view.

If the Ptolemies had not pursued their aggressive acquisitions policy in Alexandria, confiscating books from private readers and failing to return scrolls borrowed from other repositories for copying, many of the lost works might well have survived. But the Ptolemies didn't see their library as a universal repository devoted to the preservation of liberal learning, however much our cherished origin myths may have us believe it was so. Libraries are as much about losing the truth—satisfying the inner barbarians of princes, presidents, and pretenders—as about discovering it. The loss of libraries is often enough the product of the fear, ignorance, and greed of their supposed benefactors and protectors. The willful ineptitude of bureaucracies throughout history plays its role as well. Threatening images of invading barbarians may be a salve in such instances; only catastrophe can provide the drama that acts as a drug against the existential horror of decadence and decline.

The libraries of Alexandria probably shared a modest fate, moldering slowly through the centuries as people grew indifferent and even hostile to their contents. Ancient Greek, never a linguistic monolith in any case, became incomprehensible to Alexandrians of the Christian era with their mixture of Coptic, Aramaic, Hebrew, Latin, and Koine, or demotic Greek. Ignored by the generations to whom they were indecipherable, the scrolls would have been damaged by alternating periods of moisture and aridity, eaten by the troublesome fauna and flora that have evolved especially to live in the library, stolen, lost, and, yes, burned. They were replaced by writings of the Fathers and Doctors of the church and by the thinning literature of the declining Roman world. The lens of retrospect compresses the millennia, places Theodosius (sixth century A.D.) on the same ground occupied by Cleopatra and Archimedes (who lived in the first and second century B.C., respectively). What happened to the books of Alexandria? Their true fate is discernible to librarians: many, many centuries happened to them—too many for their inevitable dispersal and disappearance to be staved off, no matter who held the monopoly on papyrus, no matter whose mobs rioted in the streets, no matter which emperors set fires.

A CENTURY AFTER Alexander encircled his city with a wall of flour, the Qin emperor Shi Huangdi began to connect his far-flung forts with the stone embattlements that would become the Great Wall of China. According to the chronicles, Shi Huangdi next undertook perhaps the most extensive book burning the world has ever known. His aim, the same chronicles tell, was to destroy all Chinese literature, all history, all philosophy written before the founding of his dynasty. When he died, six thousand terra cotta warriors accompanied him, buried together in a vast funerary complex near the modern-day city of Xian, in central China. As the chronicles have it, though, he didn't extend the luxury of effigy to the traditional Confucian scholars: they were buried in person when their books were burned.

The First August Emperor (*Shi Huangdi*, the title he chose for himself) emerged in the third century B.C., at the end of what is now called the Warring States period, before a unified China existed. His father was the king of Qin, a mountainous state in China's northwestern borderlands, scarcely different in terrain or culture from the lands of the "barbarians" from whom Shi Huangdi would one day wall off his domain. The emperor-to-be was born Chao Cheng, when his father was a hostage in the state of Chou. Perhaps this fact explains the son's tenacity in wiping out not only the Chou but China's five other independent states. The elite of those states were Confucian traditionalists, to whom personal virtue and appeal to tradition were the bases of civil society and royal authority. The leaders and scholars of Qin, by contrast, saw men as selfish and inherently opposed to the power of the ruler, which they enforced through the harshest and most assertive methods. Chao Cheng assumed his father's throne at the age of thirteen; he kept "the black-haired people," as he called China's masses, in a constant state of war for the next twenty-six years, until at last the six kings fell and their states came under his own firm rule.

However mythologized the chronicler's accounts of Shi Huangdi's exploits may be, there can be little doubt that he was colorful in his megalomania. The reach of his power, he believed,

extended to all of nature and even to heaven. When he was climb-
ing with his retinue down Mount Tai, a storm blew up. The royal
company found shelter beneath a tree; in gratitude, the emperor
rewarded the tree by making it a feudal lord, "a gentleman of the
fifth rank." Another time he was traveling downriver when a wind
nearly upset the royal barge. Learning that they had just passed a
shrine to the memory of a princess, he blamed her spirit for nature's
infraction. In retribution, he ordered the mountain on which the
temple stood stripped of trees and painted red.

Attracted to this eccentric new power, traditional scholars
swarmed the imperial court, warning the emperor of the risks he
faced in failing to follow the examples set by the kings of antiquity.
But they grossly miscalculated; for in doing so, they offended him
whose dynasty represented a new dawn, unprecedented in power
and pretension. His chancellor, Li Si—whose Legalist scholarship
was snubbed by the Confucians—took the opportunity to strike at
his own rivals. "Now your majesty has initiated this great undertak-
ing, establishing merit that will last 10,000 generations. This is not
the sort of thing that a stupid Confucianist would understand!" The
chancellor had his emperor's ear. As the chronicler from the first
century B.C., Sima Qian, tells it (in Burton Watson's translation), Li
Si pressed his case:

> In the past the empire was fragmented and in confusion and no one
> was able to unite it. Therefore the feudal rulers rose up side by side,
> all of them declaiming on antiquity in order to disparage the pres-
> ent, parading empty words in order to confuse the facts. Men prided
> themselves on their private theories and criticized the measures
> adopted by their superiors. . . . I therefore request that all records of
> the historians other than those of the state of Qin be burned.

Sima Qian assures his readers that the emperor agreed wholeheart-edly: "an imperial decree," he relates dispassionately, "granted approval of the proposal."

They would have burned well. Paper was not invented in China until the second century A.D. While silk was often used as a writing medium, books in ancient China were typically compiled on strips of wood or bamboo, sewn together like venetian blinds with silken thread. Each strip contained a single row of characters, read vertically; the thin vertical form of these early books helped to determine the flow of Chinese writing on paper centuries later (though Chinese historically has followed a variety of patterns on the page). The books themselves were rolled up tightly for storage. An imperial report from the first century B.C. (almost two hundred years after the burning of the books) mentions the ample space afforded for book storage in the palace precincts, which contained 484 duplicate bundles of the works of Kuan Tzu alone.

Not long after the alleged burning of the books, a pair of divin-ers grew dissatisfied with the emperor's prohibitions against magic and scholarship carried on outside the court. They fled, searching for themselves the herbs of immortality. Enraged, the emperor ordered a roundup of such independent "masters," a term that, as the Sinol-ogist Martin Kern relates, referred both to classical scholars and to physicians, augurs, and interpreters of dreams. According to Sima Qian, more than 460 were executed. The word he uses, *keng*, is usu-ally translated as "executed," though it literally means "buried alive." Sima Qian's term for the event, terse and to the point, would be invoked by generations of Confucian scholars as the *fengshu kengru*, the burning of books and burial of scholars.

This is the story that attracted Jorge Luis Borges, who was charmed in his curious way by the juxtaposition of burning books and building walls. In his essay "The Wall and the Books," he discusses how

> these two vast undertakings—the five or six hundred leagues of
> stone against the barbarians, and the rigorous abolition of history,
> that is, of the past—[which] were the work of the same person and
> were, in a sense, his attributes, inexplicably satisfied and, at the
> same time, disturbed me. . . . Perhaps the wall was a metaphor; per-
> haps Shih Huang Ti condemned those who loved the past to a
> work as vast as the past, as stupid and as useless.

The story has been employed, too, as a kind of allegory of the Cultural Revolution; scholars who supported the government of the People's Republic have touted it as a salutary example of a regime dealing properly with a reactionary elite. It's no wonder that the story of Shi Huangdi's burning of books is, like that of the library of Alexandria, largely mythical.

Although some destruction of books and persecution of scholars took place, it seems likely Sima Qian exaggerated its extent. In any case, the Qin approach to books was altogether more complex than the chronicler's tale of the *fengshu kengru* might suggest. In a 1975 excavation of a Qin burial, one coffin was found to contain, jumbled among the bones, some eleven hundred written bamboo strips. They were from legal texts; the deceased was probably a Legalist scholar. Another scholar was laid to rest with his diary rolled up and placed like a pillow beneath his head. Books were important to the Qin elite, and they continued to read and write them throughout the first emperor's reign. Had it been entirely otherwise, it seems unlikely that scholars' burials would have so celebrated their relation to books.

Not only did scholars continue to be active in the reign of Shi Huangdi, but he did not scruple to use their learning in celebration of his rule. Between 219 and 210 B.C., the new emperor toured the newly conquered eastern states. On these tours, he made pilgrimages with his closest advisers to mountaintops, where they erected stelae, or stone pillars, bearing inscriptions extolling the virtues of his rule. The seven surviving stelae texts are formally composed and densely allusive to the traditions of Confucian scholarship. Martin Kern, whose translations of the stelae texts are as authoritative as they are graceful, can trace nearly every one of the terse, four-syllable lines of the inscriptions to traditional sources. The inscription on Mount Lang-yeh states, "Diligently he labors on the principal tasks. / He exalts agriculture, eliminates peripheral [occupations]." Kern argues that this perhaps refers to Shi Huangdi's suppression of the scholars. In his stelae at least, Shi Huangdi made no attempt to erase the authority of history and the texts it handed down; on the contrary, he constitutes the story of his rule out of the very literature he is reputed to have burned.

According to Kern, the presence of Confucian allusions in these stone inscriptions, as well as in Qin court poetry and hymns found inscribed on bells, jars, and other bronze vessels, points to the survival of the old scholarship through the reign of Shi Huangdi. The burned books were likely those held by private scholars unwilling to submit to Qin authority over intellectual matters; these, too, are the scholars, diviners, and other freelance intellectuals who found themselves buried like so many clay soldiers. The emperor appears to have sought control not only over classical learning but over all intellectual work; the work of doctors and diviners operating outside imperial restrictions would have presented a clear threat to the new emperor's secular authority. Shi Huangdi seems to have realized what the Ptolemies in Egypt had discovered: that a monopoly on intellectual resources was as important to rule as imperial control over the production of rice and silk. The Confucian canon emerged from the Qin dynasty tighter and more coherent than it was at the start—though we may reasonably fault the emperor's choice of editorial method.

The fate of the Qin dynasty was not glorious. Shi Huangdi died while returning from a campaign against peasant uprisings. Just three years later, his son and heir was murdered. The empire dissolved for a time into struggles among peasant chiefs and feudal dukes. The leaders of the peasants who ultimately founded the next dynasty, the Han, followed the Qin in their ferocity. When the future emperor Liu Ji's father was kidnapped by a rival who threatened to boil him alive, the leader showed his coarse mettle by requesting a bowl of soup made from the resulting stock.

Once the Han dynasty was founded and its rivals extinguished, however, its dukes and ministers went looking for legitimacy in scholarship and contemplation. Confucian scholars provided it, arguing that the Han's authority must rest in their defense of that classical scholarship which Shi and his chancellor, Li Si, had both suppressed and exploited. These scholars would provide more than ritual incantations and court counsel; they would provide a legitimation for the usurpers as well. The many strengths of the first Qin emperor—his consolidation of authority, his bringing of peace to the warring states, his much trumpeted standardization of weights, measures, coin, and even axle sizes—were obscured, while his viciousness, which hardly distinguished him from other kings, was reinterpreted as without precedent or pretext. Lu Jia, the new emperor's chief minister, argued in his report to the new emperor that it was through such viciousness that the Qin had lost their empire, and that only by adopting the ways of the Confucian sage—which presumably did not include occasional meals of paternal stew—could the Han hope to inaugurate an infinite reign. Yet Lu Jia himself made no reference to the story that in later times character-

ized the rule of the first Qin emperor—the *fengshu kengru*, or burning of books and burying of scholars.

Later Confucian scholars, jostling for prominence in the
empire's service, sought to establish a textual tradition reaching
back to Confucius himself, through the cataclysms of the Warring
States period and the Qin rise to power. It was given to Sima Qian,
a Han-dynasty Confucian with an intense desire to discredit all that
Shi Huangdi had done, to tell the final version. The Chinese
Herodotus, Sima Qian wrote the great *Shiji*, a history of imperial
China that was universal in scope. Although it would not be the
biggest book in China—the encyclopedia *Yung Lo Ta Tien* of the fifteenth century A.D. comprised more than eleven thousand volumes—it was very nearly universal in size as well. On the narrow
strips of bamboo, it was enormous; as the Sinologist Grant Hardy
describes it, "it would have been impossible to hold the original
Shiji in one's hands; in fact, it would have taken a cart to contain
it." In it, Sima Qian related the story of the chancellor's decree; he
told the tale of the 460 scholars buried alive. Thus was the colorful
story born, a mixture of reshuffled facts and practical fantasies.
Through his story of the *fengshu kengru*, the biblioclasm of Qin,
Sima Qian helped restore scholarship to imperial authority, and
allowed it to enjoy an authority and a freedom it would otherwise
have lacked. Without a story of burned books, many more books
might never have been written.

Sima Qian's flimsy bamboo and ink did what Shi Huangdi's
stone stelae and bronze bells could not: it told the story of the dawn
of an empire, and it made that story stick. In a sense, the intellectual
history of medieval China is the story of a struggle between the
ephemeral and the durable—between stone and bronze inscriptions
of the state and the calligraphy on silk and bamboo of the scholars
and the priests. The latter would be persuasive because the scribes

kept writing, because they ran the archives, and because they knew the stories best and wouldn't stop telling them.

As for Sima Qian, his most subtle defamation of the First August Emperor comes when he praises him. For where he does so it is in terms of comparison to past rulers of Qin and the emperors of antiquity. Of course, such praises followed the conservative form of classical scholarship, but given Shi Huangdi's ambivalent relation to the classics, such traditional praise carried an ironic undertone. No confirmation of the heavenly authority of the Han, however, could help their author in the end. Having unsuccessfully defended a vilified minister from defamatory charges, he was given a choice: he could suffer castration or execution. So Sima Qian became a eunuch and had to bury his own book (which was a library unto itself) in the ground in order to protect it from imperial authorities.

Even in the Han dynasty, despite the value it placed on classical learning, threats to books and scholars persisted. In response to such threats, scholars sought a medium more permanent than the bamboo strips and silk sheets on which writing was typically preserved. In the centuries between the rise of the Qin and the invention of paper, scholars and priests founded new kinds of libraries across China, libraries impervious to fire and burial. The Fang shan collection of Buddhist sutras founded in A.D. 550 in Hunan, China, for instance, is an enormous library. In its 4.2 million words it comprises one of the most complete and authoritative collections of Buddhist scripture in Chinese. But there is not one book in the Fang shan library—not one silk scroll, not one shred of paper. Instead, the words of the sutras are carved, in the finest book hand with characters one inch high, on stone stelae and the walls of caves. Of course, stone carvings of writing were nothing new, as Shi Huangdi's own mountaintop stelae attest. But the systematic collection and preservation of classical texts on stone was a unique devel-

Priests burning Aztec books (in the clutches of the cleric at the far right).
Tlaxcala Codex 13. Glasgow University Library, Hunterian Collection 242.
By permission of Glasgow University Library.

opment. The Buddhists, whose body of teachings emerged in the
first century A.D., late in the Han dynasty, realized that carved texts
allowed rubbings to be made, providing ready copies for the faith-
ful. Their stone libraries and "stele forests" are found today throughout China; the stones black with the ink from rubbings taken
throughout the centuries, representing surely millions and perhaps

billions of cheaply made copies of books. Though Taoists and Confucians shared the practice, the carving of stelae was particularly important to Buddhists, whose proselytization later motivated the invention of printing (the techniques of which were pioneered in China before the eleventh century), which prefigures, and mirrors, the significance of its rediscovery in fifteenth-century Germany and its importance to the progress of the Reformation and European culture.

MYTHICAL OR REAL, biblioclasms have their reasons. Often they are accidental, as when Caesar torched his ships in the harbor at Alexandria. Purposeful book burnings are of two kinds: they may be attempts at revision, such as with Shi Huangdi; another example comes from the emergence of Islam, when the Koran's adherents burned other religious texts deemed unauthoritative. In this case, the burning was a kind of sacrament; believers consigned the books to the flames almost reverentially, lest they contain words of truth hidden among the pages of error. Or books may be burned in order to erase their authors and readers from history, as the conquest of Mexico shows.

After Tenochtitlán fell to Hernán Cortés, the conquest of Mexico became a battle of the books: namely, that of the written histories of the Mexica versus the Christian Bible. The technology of the book had arisen in Mesoamerica at least a thousand years before the arrival of Columbus, and it had achieved in that time extraordinary subtlety and sophistication. In Mayan writing—probably the most complex of the Mesoamerican systems—a glyph could be a calendrical designation, a name, or even a phonetic symbol for a syllable. The materials varied, from stones to leather and other materials. The Aztecs wrote their books on specially prepared deerskin or native paper made from the fibers of the agave plant; the script was painted in vibrant colors by means of fine brushes, and covers were often made of jaguar skin.

In the centuries since the conquest, scholars often have disparaged the hieroglyphic writing of Mesoamerica, calling it "less advanced" than Egyptian hieroglyphs. But as codices and inscriptions continue to be deciphered, it's increasingly clear that earlier European critics didn't have their terms straight. The iconic script known in Nahuatl as *tlacuilolli*, for instance, is said by Gordon Brotherston to "fuse into one visual statement what for us are the separate concepts of letter, art, and mathematics." Conceptually, too, in Mesoamerican writing, outward simplicity conceals hidden depths. Most Aztec histories, for instance, were composed on the plan of the most fundamental of all Mesoamerican ordering systems: the calendar. But these calendrical annals incorporated history, divination, biography, and myth, reflecting the world of Mesoamerican religion and the minutiae of its history. Other genres existed as well: a remarkable herbal (a book containing names and descriptions of useful plants) and Aztec imperial tax statutes are among the handful of pre-conquest works to have survived. But the Aztec libraries consisted chiefly of the calendrical annals, which were revered for the religious lore and divinatory power they imparted.

Recognizing the importance of these books to the Mexican priests and nobility, the conquerors tracked down and burned all the Aztec painted books they could find. The Mexican scribes knew that their history was imperiled. They continued producing codices in secret; the Spanish did not root out the last scribal colleges in mountainous Oaxaca for another century. But the Spanish fathers charged with converting Mesoamericans were implacable. Unable to separate the historical value of the Aztec books from the religious threat they posed, they burned books wherever they were found.

It took only a few years for them to recognize their folly. The lost Aztec books contained information on the history, ethnography, and languages of Mesoamerica that would prove crucial to christianizing the cultures of Mexico. Within a few years of the conquest, according to the groundbreaking Mexican historian Miguel León-Portilla, missionaries began teaching Aztec nobles to use the Roman alphabet to write the Nahuatl language; a few of the scribes they trained went on to collaborate with Europeans in the production of books that synthesized the pre-Columbian hieroglyphic script with European phonetic writing. The greatest of these works was written by the Franciscan Bernardino de Sahagún, whose *Historia general de las cosas de Nueva España* is a vast encyclopedia of Mesoamerican civilization, treating Aztec history, ethnobotany, religion, and medicine. A unique synthesis of the Mesoamerican and European traditions of the manuscript book, its fairest copy is known as the Florentine Codex—for it resides in the Laurentian Library in Florence, Italy, founded by Cosimo de' Medici and designed by Michelangelo.

But the Spanish were not the first to burn the books of the Valley of Mexico; the Aztecs had discovered on their own how to bind books and how to destroy them. The ancestors of the Aztec rulers of Tenochtitlán had been the Mexica—nomadic tribes who had swarmed out of the north barely one hundred years before the Spanish conquest. As the Mexica cemented their control and began to extend their influence throughout the region, their priests realized that the old chronicles of wandering and savagery would not do. The Mexica quickly transformed themselves into the Aztecs, creating a new order of nobility, new taxes, and a new system of theocracy for the Valley of Mexico. Such sweeping transformations called for the support of a new history as well. And so the old books were gathered and burned. The decision came from Itzcóatl himself, the first Aztec emperor, who took a hand in the composition of the new story, writing hymns to the revised Aztec past. The new books left no doubt as to the ancient origins of the Aztec claim to power. Nor was it the last chance the Aztec scribes would have to revise their history. When they began to collaborate with priests like Father Bernardino to re-create the chronicles of the lost empire, they would insert into their histories retroactive omens and oracles that "foretold" the coming of the conquistadores in mythologized terms. Thus did they gratify their new rulers' vanity, even as they validated the power of the complex, brutal religion they had been forced to abandon.

BIBLIOCLASMS accidental, revisionary, and comprehensive: Rome knew them all. Its mythology even offers the possibility of a civilization finding its birth in the burning of books. Among the tales of Rome's origins is that of the Cumaean Sibyl, a prophetess who authored books of oracles that predicted the glory of Rome, only to burn them by her own hand. As a maiden, she had spurned the smitten god Apollo, who exacted his revenge by giving her the immortality she craved—without eternal youth. So she aged through the ages, ostracized for her bountiful warts and her bowed back. Apollo apparently took pity on her, though, and granted her the gift of prophecy. She sat in a cave in the Hill of Cumae, passing the years by writing down her oracular visions on palm leaves. In Virgil's telling, Aeneas came ashore at Cumae, where he visits the Sibyl, who delivers to him her awesome and terrible prophecy of a future Rome. Michelangelo included her image among the prophets in the Sistine Chapel; he shows her with turbanned head, her face deeply creased, but cradling her prophetic book in arms thick and supple as a stonecutter's.

My favorite image of the Cumaean Sibyl is down the hall from Michelangelo's masterpiece, in the Vatican's Salone Sistino. This glittering room was once the heart of the Vatican Library; in fact, the halls through which visitors now exit the Sistine Chapel *were* the library, and the painted wooden cabinets that line the walls ("Do you think they keep the priestly vestments in these?" I heard a fellow tourist ask his wife) once contained the books. The fresco in the Salone Sistino is one of a series depicting great libraries and book burnings of antiquity; it shows the Sibyl as she offers to sell nine books of prophecy—her visions, gathered and inscribed in books of palm leaf—to the early Roman king Tarquin the Bold. When Tarquin dismisses her terms, she throws the first three books on the fire, and offers the remaining six at the original price. Again the king refuses. When the Sibyl of Cumae throws three more volumes on the fire, the slow-witted Tarquin is finally impressed, and pays her price for the remaining three books. This is the scene the Vatican fresco presents, with Tarquin anguishing over the books piled into the brazier while a strangely youthful Sibyl stands insouciant before him. The myth ends with the remaining books installed in the Roman Forum, where they would be consulted by Rome's emperors in desperate times until the fourth century A.D. At some point, however, they disappeared; perhaps they were simply lost, or perhaps some smiling barbarian or Roman general amused himself by consigning the last three volumes to their sisters' fate. Today, the precise contents of the Sibylline Books remain a mystery; from a few snippets quoted in other sources, they seem to have consisted of vague aphorisms written down in Greek—cold comfort to an emperor faced with plague, assassination, or invasions of barbarians.

Although the Sibyl is mythical, her books were real enough. Installed first in the Roman Forum, they later resided in a hollow space beneath the statue of Apollo in Augustus's great Palatine Library. In truth, they marked the beginning of Rome's libraries. But until the time of Julius Caesar, books in Rome were largely in private hands; and the owners of great libraries, like Cicero, shared them only with friends and fellow elites. The notion of a public library very much like our own is the invention of Caesar, who had planned one for the city just before his assassination. After Caesar's death, his supporter Asinius Pollio and the writer Varro (whose treatise on library administration, the *De bibliothecis*, does not survive) took up the cause, building Rome's first public library in the Forum around 39 B.C. Following Caesar's wishes, they built a library with two reading rooms—one for Latin books, another for Greek—decorated with statues of appropriate poets and orators. This is the pattern all subsequent Roman libraries take, from the great imperial repositories of Augustus and Trajan to the more modest public libraries and to the little collections of the provincial cities. It marks a strict departure from the Greek model, with its prototype at Alexandria, which had no reading rooms as such. The bilingual nature of the Roman library expressed the Mediterranean heritage to which Rome laid claim, while the emphasis on the reader's experience gives proof of its republican origins.

In libraries as with everything else, Augustus, Rome's first true emperor, both followed Caesar and strove to best him. Once his rivals were safely dead, Augustus set to transforming Rome into an imperial city; later he boasted that he had found Rome brick and left it marble. Among his marble edifices was the great Palatine Library, adjoining his temple of Apollo, as well as a second, later library in the nearby colonnade he built in memory of his sister, Octavia. Of this second one nothing remains. But the remnants of the Palatine Library provide a picture of imperial libraries, with its two side-by-side reading rooms, with niches in the walls for the placement of *armaria*, or doored wooden bookcases, which housed the scrolls. Deeper alcoves provided space for statues. The Roman biographer of emperors Suetonius agrees with Virgil that the Sibylline Books were brought to this temple, where they were installed beneath the statue of their fickle patron, Apollo.

Like Augustus, subsequent emperors each included a library or two in his imperial building projects. Of these perhaps the greatest was Trajan's, whose library departed from the side-by-side floor plan of the others. His two reading rooms faced each other, communicating through screened colonnades. In the court between them stood the Column of Trajan, the monument for which that emperor is most famous. Though it seems incredible now, this man of war and intrigue placed the supreme memorial to his life of action in the middle of a library.

The emperors didn't only put libraries in their private palaces and temples; they also gave them to the people of Rome. In Augustus's reign, public baths—part of the "bread and circus" largesse with which the imperial city contented the masses—included libraries among their amenities. Although these libraries followed the imperial layout with opposed reading rooms for the two languages, it's likely that they contained more familiar and classical literary works and fewer arcane legal, scientific, and medical treatises than the royal collections did. Whereas the books of Alexandria are reputed to have met their end in the furnaces of public baths, the public library itself seems to have originated in the bathhouse.

The development and spread of libraries throughout the Roman world was especially remarkable given the decentralized and extra-official character of Roman intellectual life. In the public sphere, the pursuit of knowledge, like the pursuit of wealth or power, was a matter of private associations and casual relations among people. Unlike the Ptolemies, the Qin dynasty, or the Aztec nobility, Roman emperors rarely sought direct control over the life of the mind. As the classicist Elizabeth Rawson has pointed out,

Rome lacked schools and universities (many Roman elite went to Greece for schooling); no formal competitions existed for writers and artists, as they had in Greece; nor did the state pay the salaries of engineers, physicians, teachers, or other professionals, who depended on the patronage of individual senators or the imperial house. In this light, the flourishing libraries of Rome are unique: they are the nearest thing Rome had to incorporated, official cultural institutions as we know them today.

For the individual, likewise, literature was never a vocation, but merely a hobby; the writing of history, drama, or lyric poetry was suitable only to a public man's *otium*, or leisure time. But as the career of Marcus Tullius Cicero shows, this does not lessen the importance of literature and libraries in Roman public life. Cicero was the foremost example of the Roman man of letters; his career as a senator, lawyer, and republican official spanned Rome's most turbulent era, in which civil wars destroyed the republic and ushered in the empire, and his letters are a record of Rome's turmoil as important as that of any historian. But it was his talents as an orator that raised him to the heights of the senatorial elite. To Cicero, public life and letters were one. The history of republican Rome and its founding families provided him not only with edifying stories to occupy his leisure hours but with crucial political ammunition as well. Son of a wealthy citizen of common origins, he was frequently shocked at the willful ignorance the scions of Rome's great families showed of their own history. His letters to friends and clients, by contrast, often contain carefully considered requests for information from the senatorial archives.

Like all Roman writers, Cicero expended a great deal of energy buying and copying books and building his library. In this he benefited from the help of Tyrannio, Rome's greatest teacher and scholar, whose own library was reputed to hold some thirty thousand scrolls; from his friends, especially Titus Pomponius Atticus, whose 416 letters from Cicero survive in modern editions; and especially from his many educated Greek slaves. In Rome, many of the tasks of scholarship, from teaching to copying and editing and librarianship, were handled by educated slaves, most of them Greek, who were among the most prized members of any elite household. In this manuscript culture, a slave-owning man of letters was not only a writer, a critic, and a reader—he became of necessity a publisher as well, of his own works and those of others. Though Rome supported a thriving book trade, discriminating readers knew that the texts offered in the bookstalls were often hopelessly corrupt. Cicero and his friends provided each other with carefully copied editions of their own works and those from their collections. Cicero did so when he compiled the *Academia*, his great anthology of Academic philosophy, for the writer Varro's use. He recounts its production to his friend Atticus in a letter of June 24, 45 B.C.:

> I have taken the whole Academy from highly aristocratic personages . . . ; and from two books I have put it into four. They are bigger than the old ones, yet I have removed a good deal. . . . As for the work, unless my share of *amour propre* deceives me, it has turned out better than anything in its genre now existing, even in Greek. I am sure you will take a philosophical view of the waste of your copyists' labour on the treatise on Academic doctrine which you already have. This one will be far finer, more concise, better.

His speeches before the Senate, like his books, are "far finer, more concise, better" than those of his peers, and knit together with a complex and eclectic rhetorical style that was Cicero's alone. He used his unmatched talents as an orator to mount a persistent defense of republican Rome in the face of the advance of Julius Caesar and his rivals. Though he did not take part in Caesar's assassination, his republican sympathies were well known, and when he ran afoul of Caesar's successor Octavian—who later would be called Augustus—he was tracked down and killed. His hands and head were lopped off and put on display at the site of his greatest triumphs, atop the speaker's rostrum in the hall of the Senate.

As the republic became an empire, though, Cicero's beloved libraries flourished. Even amid the chronic fires that plagued Rome, they were maintained into the fourth century. The city's great conflagration of A.D. 64 (during which Nero supposedly fiddled as the city burned) claimed the Palatine Library. Domitian restored it; he did the same for Augustus's Octavian Library when it burned. This is remarkable, given Domitian's lack of interest in letters. Of Domitian, Suetonius writes, "All liberal studies in the beginning of his empire he neglected; albeit he took order to repair the libraries consumed with fire, to his exceeding great charges, making search from all parts for the copies of books lost, and sending as far as Alexandria to write and correct them."

The splendor of the empire persisted long into its decline, and even Christian Romans as late as the fifth century would visit each other's villas to relive the splendor of bygone days. The prolific epistoler Sidonius Apollinaris, in a letter to his friend Donidius written about A.D. 430, describes such a scene: the shouts of youth sporting on the fields, the chatter of dice, and laughter pealing out in secluded rooms. He finds his greatest joy, however, in the villa library, where he discovers

> books in any number ready to hand; you might have imagined yourself looking at the shelves of a professional scholar or at the tiers in the Athenaeum or at the towering presses of the book-

sellers. The arrangement was such that the manuscripts near the ladies' seats were of a devotional type, while those among the gentlemen's benches were works distinguished by the grandeur of Latin eloquence; the latter, however, included certain writings of particular authors which preserve a similarity of style though their doctrines are different; for it was a frequent practice to read writers whose artistry was of a similar kind—here Augustine, there Varro, here Horace, there Prudentius.

Sidonius's description provides evidence of changes in the uses of books, even amid the continued appreciation of "the grandeur of Latin eloquence." First of all, there is now space for the once dissident books of those Gibbon calls the Galileans. Sidonius himself was a devout Christian, as were most of his fellow elite by this time. But that didn't stop them from appreciating the rhetorical perspicacity of such pagan authors as Varro and Horace. In the fourth century, Saint Jerome could still dream of being damned for idolatry for his devotion to the pagan classics, yet the proscription against the pagans even a few decades later was not so great as to give Sidonius and his friends pause.

The fact that "devotional books" are placed near the women's seating gives another view of the sociology of reading in the late empire. In pagan times, women had not often been offered much in the way of an education. Cicero's daughter, Tullia, was a rare exception: privately tutored, she was called *doctissima*, or "most learned," by her father in his moving essay *Consolatione*, written upon her death. When women did receive education, through either their own industry or the unorthodox methods of their parents, they tended to favor philosophy and mathematics over literature; for the latter was a masculine and practical subject, tuned to the needs of public discourse in the Senate. This metaphysical, mystical reading perhaps prepared Roman women to be more receptive to Christian thought, and to prize meditative works over the florid rhetoric of the poets and historians.

Finally, we can imagine that, among the many scrolls in the library Sidonius visited, there were a fair number of books as we know them today. Christians introduced the codex, or bound book, to Rome from the homelands of the early church in Palestine, Egypt, and Greece. Based on portfolios of wax-covered ivory or wood that literate Romans had long carried as a kind of notebook, pages of papyrus and vellum were first bound together in similar fashion in the Christian era. A mosaic in Ravenna, which dates from Sidonius's time, shows a traditional Roman *armarium,* or bookcase, filled with codices lying flat with their covers upturned, their titles clearly showing. They were the Gospels: the codex was still a distinctly Christian medium.

Codices are not only much easier to read than scrolls; they are easier to store, too. Though their materials are every bit as subject to decay as the papyrus used in scrolls, their stable position on the library shelf helps ensure a longer life with fewer repairs. They are also easier to organize than scrolls, which would one day permit libraries to attain far greater complexity than in antiquity. But the codex could not save private libraries like the one Sidonius describes from ultimate disappearance; in the centuries of deprivation and disorder that attended the decline of Rome, books suffered along with everything else.

In addition to the ravages of emperors, and barbarians, and angry mobs, books endure natural disasters. The city of Herculaneum was buried in the rivers of ash that flowed from the eruption of Mount Vesuvius in A.D. 79 (the same eruption that destroyed, and preserved, Pompeii). Excavations in the eighteenth century revealed a room in the famous Villa of the Papyri that contained the jumbled fragments of scrolls blackened by the fires of the eruption. Though many were too badly burned to be read, the layout of the room itself was a perfect example of a Roman library, with niches in the walls where the *armaria* were neatly installed.

The extent of the library is extraordinary: it contained some two thousand scrolls. Herculaneum was a suburb of Naples, which had grown from an early Greek colony into a deeply Hellenized, cosmopolitan city. The books of the Villa of the Papyri reflect this eclectic, literate climate—most of them were Greek works, dominated by treatises on Epicurean philosophy. Little remains of these books but carbonized chunks barely recognizable as scrolls; more than two hundred years ago excavators discarded many fragments, mistaking them for so many bits of charcoal.

An eighteenth-century Italian priest, Antonio Piaggio, invented an extraordinary machine for opening the burned scrolls: silk threads sewn to the leading edge of the papyrus are wound around an array of screws which, by their gradual tightening, peel back the burned layers; the brittle manuscript fragments are sliced away and attached to adhesive strips to strengthen and preserve them. By means of this process, a number of the scrolls have been carefully unrolled, read, and published. The majority of them, however, were thought unreadable until recently. Now a team from Brigham Young University and the Italian National Library at Naples are using digital imaging techniques to decipher the remaining fragments. Ink reflects light differently from the charred papyrus on which it is found. Spectral photography can illuminate differences between the two, rendering a lucid image of the writing. Ten thousand fragments remain; the team members believe they can decipher them all.

Long before the fall of Rome, Plato and Aristotle both came to the conclusion that there is no political system that doesn't suffer decline. As a not-so-minor corollary to this rule, it could be added that there is no library that does not ultimately disappear, leaving a lacuna for future generations to puzzle over. The tragedy of the Villa of the Papyri is the tragedy of the library throughout history: by bringing books together in one place, cultures and kings inevitably make of them a sacrifice to time. So it is with the vast majority of the libraries of antiquity, from Asia Minor to Spain, from Alexandria to Pergamum. Researchers working on the fragments of Herculaneum offer the tantalizing possibility that they may find some of the many lost works of antiquity among the fragments. But even if the last few charred characters offer up nothing new, one thing is certain: the most complete ancient library accessible to us today survived because it burned.

CHAPTER THREE

The House of Wisdom

As Rome's light receded from Gibbon's "fairest portion of the Earth," its libraries, too, began to gutter and die. Overall it was a dark time for learning, for books, and for libraries. Culturally, Roman Christians built an identity for themselves in opposition to the literature and art of pagan antiquity. As the commercial and social decline of the empire wore on, education fragmented, the sources of cash needed to buy and prepare vellum and papyrus and to sustain armies of copyists dried up, and the roads that once carried Rome's efficient post—so important to the life of the *Respublica litterarum*—fell into disrepair. Late letters show that Roman nobles had taken up the task of their own copy work, a sure sign that the once steady supply of educated slaves had dwindled.

A dim, uncertain flame still flickered, however, among early Christian monastic communities. Despite material poverty and religious mandates, the literary culture of antiquity persisted among the monks: in one anchorite community in Egypt around 600, the brethren scratched out not only scriptural passages but even lines from the *Iliad* and the *Sentences* of Menander, on *ostraca*, or potsherds. That no more suitable writing material could be found in a monastery in the homeland of papyrus may indicate the poverty of the community, although that didn't stop the monks from pursuing reading and study. But perhaps it also suggests changes in the uses of reading and writing. After the fall of the Roman Empire, writing became a perishable medium; its uses were temporary and expedient. Without the empire's hunger for stone inscription, without official decrees and speeches to put down on vellum and papyrus, little was being written for a permanent record. The monks wrote to learn to read and copy Scripture, and to exert themselves in spiritually rewarding labor. Besides that on *ostraca*, most writing in this time would have been inscribed on wax tablets, which by their nature do not survive long.

It was probably from such wax tablets that Coptic monks in Egypt had first taken the inspiration to invent, or at least to perfect, the form of the book as we know it today: the codex. The wax tablet was an important writing medium from Mesopotamian days well into the Middle Ages. It has been speculated that the English word "book" in fact comes from the Anglo-Saxon word for beech (*boc*), the favored material from which the panels of tablets were fashioned. The panels typically were carved with a shallow reservoir into which beeswax could be poured; cool, the beeswax made a soft surface into which letters could be inscribed with a sharp stylus. A vigorous rubbing quickly erased the panel—very convenient for the writer, less so for the historian; no wax-tablet literature survives. Often two such panels were joined together with cord, though some writers preferred tablets of several panels. Possibly in Egypt, scribes adapted papyrus sheets to the format of the many-paneled wax tablet, replacing the scrolls that were the staple of antiquity.

Near the town of Nag Hammadi in Egypt is the site where the monastery of Chenoboskion stood in the fourth century. In 1945, thirteen simple codices dating from the second half of the fourth century were found there, sealed in a clay jar. The texts these books contain have provided scholars with a fuller picture of the intellectual and spiritual world of the early Christians and the Gnostic sects with which they were in contact and conflict. The bindings survived as well, and they offer the best examples of the Coptic origin of the codex. The books consisted of simple folded gatherings of papyrus sheets sewn loosely into a leather cover. With their tied flaps, the Nag Hammadi codices look stylish, even by today's standards. Fancy journal books constructed exactly like those of the Nag Hammadi library can be found in any stationery store today.

And it was not only books that survived; in at least one case, the small monastic libraries preserved a whole literature as well. In the tenth century, a Syrian monastery led by Moses of Nisibis preserved some 250 manuscripts. Many of these were in Syriac, a Semitic language, close to Aramaic, which was spoken by the Nestorian community. In the Middle Ages, Syriac was a widespread language, of great importance to early Christians (Jesus, after all, spoke Aramaic). Syriac's importance was not limited to Christian theology, however. Eighth-century bilingual stone inscriptions, in Chinese and Syriac, survive in modern Xian in China. Syriac had its great poets, too, such as Ephrem of Nisibis, who wrote in forms that had their roots in the cuneiform literatures of Mesopotamia. Tenth-century Moses had collected the books of these authors and others just in time, for the invading Turks nearly destroyed the Syriac tongue along with its speakers. The language is alive today in the mouths of those surviving speakers' descendants, most of whom live in Syria, Iraq, Iran, and a diaspora spread from Turkey to western Europe. Much of what remains of Syriac literature, however, was preserved in the collection Moses made.

Medieval trends not only in librarianship but in the entire monastic way of life sprang from Cassiodorus, a Roman noble and Christian who flourished in the sixth century. Cassiodorus had served the Ostrogothic king Theodoric until the eastern emperor Justinian laid siege to Rome and brought Italy under the rule of Constantinople. Cassiodorus lived to see the destruction of the last of Rome's great libraries, the Palatine and Ulpian libraries, during the siege of the city. After the capital fell, Pope Agapetus established an important library and academy of his own; but Cassiodorus, nervous about the political role the established church had come to play, preferred to pursue the *vita contemplativa* outside of the church's struggle for power with secular authorities. At his Calabrian estate, he founded a monastery that was to set the pattern for the medieval orders to come. Southern Italy was largely saved from the travails of war Rome suffered in those years. Cassiodorus's haven, called Vivarium after nearby fishponds (evoking one of early Christianity's guiding metaphors, that of the fishes), sheltered a program of library building and manuscript making of extraordinary energy and importance. At Vivarium, early versions of the Gospels were collected that would prove crucial to the transmission of Scripture through the Middle Ages. Sacred writings were, of course, privileged, though Cassiodorus took great pains to preserve the literary legacy of Greece and Rome as well. While nine of the *armaria* in his library were devoted to theological writings, another cabinet contained books of the Greek classics. Cassiodorus had his monks work assiduously on a program of translating and copying these works. His own great work, the *Institutiones divinarum et saecularium litterarum*, helped put in place the epistemology of medieval Europe. A kind of encyclopedia, it ordered and explained all of sacred and secular thought for the benefit of the monks of Vivarium. In Cassiodorus's view, each side of culture mirrored the other in a set of hierarchies that ranged, on the one hand, from the Bible through the writings of the Fathers of the church down to latter-day commentaries and, on the other hand, from the heights of Homer through the orators, dramatists, and historians of antiquity. This image of literature as a diptych of mirrored orderings of the divine and the worldly helped organize the libraries of the Middle Ages, down to great Renaissance libraries like that of the Vatican.

As for Cassiodorus's own library, its fate is unknown. At its greatest extent, in the seventh century, however, it probably contained no more than a few hundred books. The great Irish monastery at Bobbio, in northern Italy, whose library may have been modeled on Vivarium's, in the tenth century contained 666 works. For all the aesthetic innovations in the form and illumination of books that flowed from them, medieval libraries in Europe were conservative places, where interest focused on a few venerated texts.

YET, AS THE SPIRIT of the universal library flagged in the West, it flourished in the East. Through the thousand years between the death of Alexander and the rise of Islam, despite the constant struggles between Rome and Persian rulers, Syria was the most stable home of Greek learning. When in 529 the emperor Justinian closed the school at Athens, putting learning under ecclesiastical control, Athens' exiled teachers looked for refuge to the ancient enemy of all things Greek: Persia. It was not an unlikely choice of haven; as conflict often does, the long enmity between Persia and Greece had brought the two cultures into close contact, while Alexander and his successors—not only the Egyptian Ptolemies but the Seleucid dynasty, founded in Syria by another one of Alexander's generals—

had infused Greek learning into the dominant culture of the Near East. Nestorian Christian copyists in Syria preserved the science even as they disdained the literature of the Greeks, preferring the Persian poetic tradition instead. And now the court of Noshirvan in Persia made room for the exiled teachers of Athens.

The greatest efflorescence of libraries came with the rise of Islam. Perhaps ironically, Muhammad had prized his own *illiteracy*, for the proof it gave of his authentic witness: he could not have read and received the influence of any other Scripture, nor could he have written Allah's words with his own hand. Even miraculous writing—like Yahweh's decalogical gift to Moses on Mount Sinai—would have failed to light the spark of belief among the skeptical Arabs. In *al-An`am* 6:7.9, Allah reminds Muhammad, "Had we sent down unto thee (actual) writing upon parchment, so that they could feel it with their hands, those who disbelieve would have said: This is naught else than mere magic." Instead, Allah instructs his prophet to command his followers to copy out the Koran so that they might come to believe it for themselves. With this mandate to write down the words the prophet had received from Allah, his followers became enthusiastically literate. Indeed, as their empire grew, they proved enthusiasts in everything, eager to learn from those they conquered. When the armies of Muhammad swept north out the Arabian peninsula in the seventh century, they conquered a Persia that retained the splendor of its ancient culture. The treasures of the Persian libraries—which through the centuries of conflict with Greece had filled up not only with Persian texts but with the science and philosophy of the Hellenic world—were opened up to translators. Now, under the calligraphers' hands, Greek science followed Persian poetry into Arabic. Thus began an epoch of Muslim library building that would last a thousand years, eventually delivering a shared Greek heritage to the hands of an upstart Europe.

Muslim culture and its libraries grew with astonishing speed. By the end of the eighth century, the Abbasid dynasty had made Baghdad a world center of learning. The Abbasids' predecessors, the Umayyad caliphs, had already privileged books and learning. They had built great sacred libraries at their capital in Damascus and in the al-Aqsa mosque in Jerusalem. The first Umayyad caliph, Muawiyah I, appointed a *sahib al-masahif*, or curator of books, to care for his royal library, into which went not only sacred writings but works in the liberal arts and sciences; it became a flourishing universal library along Alexandrian lines. But when the Abbasids overthrew the Umayyads in the east, books began to flow toward their new capital at Baghdad.

The speedy rise of Arab civilization is exemplified in the story of the Banu Musa, three brothers who served the Abbasid court as mathematicians and astronomers. Little is known about the lives of the three brothers, who together authored the *Kitab marifat masakhat al-ashkal*, or *Book of the Measurement of Plane and Spherical Figures*, one of the foundational texts of Arabic mathematics. The details of their biography, however, paint a tantalizing picture of one family's rise. Their father, Musa ibn Shakir, was an infant when the first Abbasid prince rose to power (the name Banu Musa simply means "sons of Musa"). In his early adulthood, he made his living as a highwayman, until the emergent power of the new caliphate persuaded him to pursue a safer livelihood. Perhaps he had relied on favorable stars to ensure his success in robbery, for he now set himself the more peaceable pursuit of astrology. Success in this new career brought him to the attention of the prince al-Mamun, who seized the caliphate from his brother in 813. When the old thief died, the caliph assumed guardianship of his three intellectually precocious sons, whom he appointed scholars to the royal House of Wisdom. At once a library, a school, and a research center, the House of Wisdom answered all the needs of the intellectually gifted young men. Thus in one generation, the family of Musa ibn Shakir rose from petty crime to the heights of academic power.

Abbasid Baghdad was an extraordinary place for boys of the Banu Musa's talent to come of age. The House of Wisdom was the center of translation, compilation, and comparison of the wisdom of the peoples under Muslim rule from India to the Iberian peninsula. The Arabic translator of Euclid, al-Hajjaj, worked there alongside al-Khwarizmi, inventor of algebra, from whose name we take the word "algorithm." Reading Hindu mathematical treatises collected in the library at the House of Wisdom, al-Khwarizmi adapted the Hindu numbering system to suit his own purposes, giving birth to the Arabic numerals we use today.

The Arabs, Nestorians, and Jews at work in Baghdad provided the three young brothers with the finest education that could be had, and when in their time they joined the House of Wisdom, they put their brilliance as mathematicians and astronomers to work for four successive caliphs. Together, they made strides that could be achieved only in a universal library like that found in the House of Wisdom. In their work, they extended the methods of Archimedes and Eudoxus; by applying a finely honed sense of number to the study of Greek geometry, they became the first to think of surfaces and spaces in numerical terms. By marrying arithmetic and geometry, they helped lay the foundations upon which Western science would eventually be built. In addition to producing their famous treatise, the brothers measured the solar year with unprecedented accuracy, designed irrigation canals, and made innovative astronomical findings from their housetop observatory. They were at the top of the Muslim intellectual world, a demimonde as riven with strife as the university is today.

The fourth caliph the brothers served, al-Mutawakkil, was not so tolerant of scholarly rivalry as his predecessors, and he favored the bridge-building, canal-digging Banu Musa over their antagonists. When the brothers clashed with the philosopher al-Kindi, the caliph empowered his favorite scientists to have the scholar beaten and to confiscate his library.

Despite such prejudiced clashes, however, books, libraries, and the arts would flourish under the Umayyads until their empire fell to invading Mongols some five hundred years later.

Much of Western book culture owes its heritage to Islam. The conquerors learned well from their new subjects, taking the forms and crafts of the book and raising them to new heights. From their Chinese prisoners, Muslims learned the art of papermaking as early as the eighth century. From Amharic scribes in Ethiopia, they borrowed the form of the codex, refining the sewn leather binding into an art of great sophistication. To the Greeks and the Romans, books had been tools, utilitarian repositories of knowledge; the scrolls they made were spare and plain, offering for aesthetic comfort only the words they contained. The calligraphers and illustrators of Islam, by contrast, made the book itself a thing of beauty, and collectors came to value the sumptuous look and feel of books as much as the writing they conveyed. In Christian Europe in the Middle Ages, connoisseurship of the illustrated book was restricted to the highest strata of society: only the nobility and the greatest of the clergy could meet the enormous cost of producing the most richly illuminated Gospels, missals, and breviaries. In the more mercantile Muslim world, by contrast, good taste in books was a prerequisite of the merchant. A tenth-century scholar complained that at a book auction in Cordova he had lost a precious volume to another bidder, who drove the price far above the actual worth of the book. Afterward, he approached the winner, who admitted that he had no idea what the book was about. He was amassing a great library to impress his business associates, and had a spot open on his shelves into which the book fit perfectly—besides, he added, the book was too beautiful to do without.

It was not only individual books but whole libraries that the Muslim elite competed to obtain. Arabic Spain had at one count seventy libraries, the largest having been established by Caliph Hakim at Cordova in 976. Cordova at that time was second only to Constantinople among European cities in size; plumbing brought water to 200,000 homes and nine hundred public baths, while the city blazed at night with public street lamps. According to the historian Ibn al-Abar, the catalog of al-Hakim's library ran to forty-four volumes, and the books themselves numbered between 400,000 and 600,000—two or three books for every house in the city, and a stunning achievement at a time when even the largest European libraries numbered in the mere hundreds of volumes. At Cordova and at Toledo, which was conquered by Christians in 1085, the Greco-Persian patrimony of Arab science was translated into Latin, the language in which it would survive the destruction of Arab intellectual culture at the hands of the Turks, the Mongols, and the Crusaders.

Great libraries sprang up everywhere in Islam's reach. The library of the Persian court was one such house of riches, as the Iranian philosopher and physician Avicenna (980–1037) testifies. Like the Banu Musa, Avicenna was a prodigy of memory and learning; by the age of ten, he had memorized not only the Koran but great quantities of poetry as well. At eighteen, he was summoned to act as royal physician to the Samanid court of Persia, where the successful cure he administered to Prince Nuh ibn-Mansur assured him of royal favor. Chief among the benefits of courtly patronage was the access he was granted to the astonishing library of the royal house. "I found there many rooms filled with books," he writes,

which were arranged in cases row upon row. One room was allot-
ted to works on Arabic philology and poetry, another to jurispru-
dence, and so forth, the books on each particular science having a
room to themselves. I inspected the catalogue of ancient Greek
authors and looked for the books which I required; I saw in this
collection books of which few people have even heard the name
and which I myself had never seen either before or since.

Avicenna's infatuation with the library must have been well
known, for when the library burned soon after his visit, the young
philosopher was accused of having set the fire in order to make himself "the sole depository of wisdom."

Whatever stories are told about the fate of the books of
Alexandria under Omar, it seems certain that they survived his
reign, since a great number of the library's books were removed to
Antioch under his successor, Omar II. When the Fatimid dynasty
succeeded the Omars in Egypt, it established its capital at Cairo,
where the caliph al-Aziz built a library as part of his own grand
"house of learning." It contained perhaps as many as 600,000 volumes, including 2,400 illuminated Korans. The rest of the books
were kept in great presses or cabinets, each of which displayed a list
of the books it contained—as well as a note naming the titles needed
to complete the collections. In 1004, the caliph al-Hakim combined
these into his collection in a "house of wisdom" of his own, reputed
to contain some 1.5 million books. But in 1068, with the Turks
approaching, the vizier Abu al-Faraj sold twenty-five camel-loads of
books to pay his army, getting 100,000 dinars for the lot. The Turkish army defeated him a few months later and disposed of the rest of
the collection in its own way, stripping the fine leather bindings to
make shoes and burying the ripped-out pages outside Cairo in a
place that would be known for generations as "the Hill of Books."

But this great efflorescence of books, learning, and libraries came to an abrupt end. The historian S. K. Padover notes that Europe's acquisition of Arabic learning through the middle of the thirteenth century occurred "just in time," for "the Mohammedan East was nearly destroyed by the invasions of the Mongols"; the Habsburg emperor Charles V ordered all books in Arabic burned when he took Tunis in 1536; and after the expulsion of the Moors from Spain in 1492 the country "was so stripped of Arabic manuscripts that, when Philip II founded the Escorial, no Arabic manuscripts could be found in the kingdom." A Moroccan ship with a cargo of books had to be seized to add the wanted Arabic titles to the royal library, but a fire in the Escorial in 1674 consumed some eight thousand Arab books. Between the thirteenth century and the fifteenth, the extraordinary libraries of the Muslim world disappeared; its conquerors—the Mongols, the Turks, and the Crusaders—did not share the love of learning that Islam had inherited from its Greco-Persian forebears.

THROUGHOUT THE MIDDLE AGES, connections persisted between the book cultures of Islam and Christian Europe. European scholars visited the great book markets of Toledo and Cordova, and during and after the Crusades, books flowed into Europe as the booty of war. In southern Italy, meanwhile, the Greek influence remained strong. At the venerable monastery of Monte Cassino, for instance, Greco-Arabic medical texts had long been copied, kept, and studied. But of the vast, tightly knit fabric of public libraries that had stretched across the Roman Empire from Spain to Greece, not a shred survived.

Like so much of classical culture, the public library had its rebirth in Florence. The title of the first modern "public" library is perhaps most often given to the library of San Marco, founded by

Cosimo de' Medici in 1444. In the terms of fifteenth-century Florence, however, the word "public" refers not to the masses but to that stage upon which the church, the nobility, and powerful mercantile families performed their roles and wielded their authority. The library at San Marco was public in this sense: that the work of scholars who used it would benefit society in a new and important way. It was public, too, in that the Medicis publicly played their manifold parts as connoisseurs, patrons, intellectuals, and princes through their gift of the library and through the particular books they chose for it. What Johan Huizinga says of the character of the Middle Ages holds true for the early Renaissance as well: "all things in life were of a proud or cruel publicity." Today public libraries are among the chief protectors of intellectual individuality and privacy. The library of San Marco was "public," really, in the sense that it was a vehicle for publicity. Of course, compared with some of the Medicis' crueler publicities, the founding of libraries seems placid and beneficent. But such beneficence played a role in ritualizing Medici power.

The historian Lisa Jardine puts the role of the library in the Medici family's rise from merchants to princes in clear terms: "One of the distinctive ways they made this transition was by turning a private interest in expenditure on rare and finely produced books (ancient and modern) into a reputation for civic benevolence. . . ." Jardine identifies the four types of books the Medicis acquired, each of which established the family's public persona in specific ways: first come "books establishing a family reputation for patronage of the humanistically arcane"; these were books that secured the Medicis' reputation as scholars and sophisticates. Next are "books establishing a family aura of probity and 'good practice'"—in other words, moral treatises and books on mores and manners, which provided a kind of genteel bibliography to validate the family's elegance. Then we have "classical tradition books which are 'precious,'" which prove the Medici patronage of the ascendant humanism. Finally come "books establishing a traceable genealogy of acquisition"—books with the autographs and ex libris of prior owners who were distinguished, significant persons, to whom the Medicis were only too happy to link their name. "What all this adds up to," Jardine argues, "is a recognisable programme of self-promotion and public commemoration of a family name, in which books simply happen to be artefacts used for such classic conspicuous consumption." In the library, the Medicis could demonstrate their intellectual integrity, their curatorial acumen, and their alignment with Renaissance values—they could perform these things publicly. The private acquisition of important books by a powerful family is the performance of their intellectual authority; the building of that collection into a library translates their action out of the medieval public performance of the household drama into an attempt to foster and influence a public sphere in the modern sense.

In the Middle Ages, access to books, and even literacy itself, was parceled out on a strict "need to know" basis. Humanism upset the political economy of reading, however, offering not only new kinds of books (namely, the rediscovered old ones) but new ways of reading them as well. No longer did princes receive their instruction primarily from the clergy; the literature of antiquity provided countless lessons for rulers and commanders of armies. In his memoir of Federigo, duke of Urbino, the Tuscan bookseller Vespasiano da Bisticci describes the ideal prince in the terms of a militant humanism: "it is difficult for a leader to excel in arms unless he be . . . a man of letters, seeing that the past is the mirror of the present. A military leader who knows Latin has a great advantage over one who does not." But in the second half of the fifteenth century, Federigo would not be the last ruler to take up reading the books of antiquity, or building libraries in which to house and care for them. Humanism drew its early energy and authority from the vanity of princes.

Vespasiano himself provides ample evidence for this: his *Lives of Illustrious Men of the XVth Century* is essentially a series of accounts of powerful men and the libraries they built. Of course, Vespasiano's own vocation needs to be taken into account here; a Florentine bookseller, he helped build the collections of the Vatican Library, the Laurentian Library, and the library of Federigo, duke of Urbino. Thus he knew the illustrious men he profiled only in terms of the books he purchased or had copied for them. But this is precisely the point: it's telling that a *bookseller* would have sufficient access to so many of the most prominent figures of Renaissance Italy that he could write significant personal memoirs of them.

And as this note of collecting rare and important books, and organizing them into libraries, plays throughout the lives of these men, we can see that in their time something did indeed change fundamentally in the nature of books and reading—and this something expresses itself in the building of libraries. Suddenly it became important to bring lots of books together in one place, to make them accessible, not only to friends, family, and sponsored artists and writers—the denizens of the private home—but to a public, to translate all those private acts of reading into public performances. In the Renaissance, as intensive private reading was rediscovered among scholars, it took on a public cast as well. It wasn't the coming of printed books a few years later that cluttered up the library; the appetite for books in large quantities was already whetted by the time the printing press made its appearance. Vespasiano captures this watershed moment in his memoir of Federigo, duke of Urbino:

> [The Duke] alone had a mind to do what no one had done for a
> thousand years or more; that is, to create the finest library since

ancient times. He spared neither cost nor labour, and when he knew of a fine book, whether in Italy or not, he would send for it. It is now fourteen or more years ago since he began the library, and he always employed, in Urbino, in Florence and in other places, thirty or forty scribes in his service. He took the only way to make a fine library like this: by beginning with the Latin poets, with any comments on the same which might seem merited; next the orators, with the works of Tully and all Latin writers and grammarians of merit; so that none of the leading writers in this faculty should be wanted. He sought also all the known works on history in Latin, and not only those, but likewise the histories of Greek writers done into Latin, and the orators as well. The Duke also desired to have every work on moral and natural philosophy in Latin, or in Latin translation from Greek.

Vespasiano's list of the books in Federigo's library goes on for pages: The Doctors of the church, the doctors of old, Greek writing done into Latin, Latin doctors in philosophy and theology, books on astrology, geometry, arithmetic, architecture, painting, sculpture, canon law, medicine, including Avicenna, Hippocrates, Galen; Averroës, Boethius, modern writers such as Dante, Petrarch, Boccaccio, complete editions of Aristotle and Plato ("written," as his Bible was, "on the finest goat-skin"), Greek poets, Ptolemy's *Cosmography*, Herodotus, Thucydides, Demosthenes, "also whatever books were to be had in Hebrew," and on and on and on. "The Duke," Vespasiano writes,

having completed this noble work at the great cost of thirty thousand ducats, . . . determined to give every writer a worthy finish by binding his work in scarlet and silver. Beginning with the Bible, as the chief, he had it covered in gold brocade, and then he bound in scarlet and silver the Greek and Latin doctors and philosophers, the histories, the books on medicine and the modern doctors, a rich and magnificent sight. In this library all the books are superlatively good, and written with the pen, and *had there been one printed volume it would have been ashamed in such company.* (emphasis added)

Big libraries didn't spring up because of the economy and efficiency of the printing press, as others would later fear; they were bound up in the appetites of dukes, and merchants, and popes for the new learning aborning in the Renaissance. For despite the challenges of the free press, the control of massed knowledge offered a new basis for their power.

Vespasiano writes of Cosimo de' Medici in these same terms. Cosimo, he says,

had a knowledge of Latin which would scarcely have been looked for in one occupying the station of a leading citizen engrossed with affairs. He was grave in temperament, prone to associate with men of high station who disliked frivolity, and averse from all buffoons and actors and those who spent time unprofitably. He had a great liking for men of letters and sought their society, chiefly conversing with the Fra Ambroglio degli Agnoli, Messer Lionardo d'Arezzo, Nicolao Nicoli, Messer Carlo d'Arezzo and Messer Poggio.

When Cosimo hired Vespasiano to furnish the library at San Lorenzo, the latter "engaged forty-five scribes and completed two hundred volumes in twenty-two months, taking as a model the library of Pope Nicolas." Here we see Vespasiano giving voice to the new kind of publicity Cosimo is seeking in his library building: his willingness to invest vast sums, to employ armies of scribes, and to select texts with unstinting rigor, all display the new commitment to learning, even as they demonstrate the real link the new learning has forged with the cultivation of power.

When he planned the San Marco Library, Cosimo took his inspiration—not to mention the books themselves—from varied sources. His explicit model again was the new Vatican Library of Pope Nicholas V, but a more important model he acquired from one of his friends and rival collectors, the humanist Niccolò Niccoli. But Niccoli was not only Cosimo de' Medici's close friend; he was in debt to him as well. Niccoli's will stipulated that any library founded on the basis of his collection should be open to "*omnes cives studiosi,*" to be managed and lent out under the guidance of a body of trustees, who would also act as curators. Cosimo was among these trustees. But Niccoli ran into money trouble before his death, in 1437, and was unable to put up the ducats needed to build a home for his books and provide for their care. Cosimo stepped in. Maneuvering against the other trustees, he secured effective control of the library in return for supplying the necessary funds; thus he moved the library into the San Marco convent, which he was having built at the time. In return, Cosimo placed a marble tablet in the library entrance declaring himself the savior of Niccoli's library and announcing his own grand vision of a public library.

Vespasiano's memoirs show how the book and the library are made things, and things commanded to be made. And for the patrons, the popes, and the princes who command their making, authorship is but a species of the work of scribes. As the classics are copied, so new works, which are also required by the patron's appetites, are produced. In the dream of the patron, however, it is he who *generates* the work; in a way, it already exists implicit within him. We must imagine him taking his author's dedication at face value. And this is how the Renaissance libraries got built: by an amassing of appetite.

✦

IT WAS THE APPETITE not of a secular prince but of the Vicar of Christ that would set the standard for library building in the Renaissance. Although he did not live to see the Vatican Library fully established, Pope Nicholas V had the idea that "for the common convenience of the learned we may have a library of all books both in Latin and Greek that is worthy of the dignity of the Pope and the Apostolic See." Nicholas's combination of common convenience and uncommon dignity nicely indexes the political impulses behind humanism.

A papal library was nothing new; as early as Cassiodorus's time, the pope had collected a library for his own use. No catalog exists for the papal collection before 1295, but we can imagine it reflected the extent and the interests of medieval monastic libraries. Pope Nicholas's notion of a library was more expansive, however: he wanted something more than the largest monastic library; he wanted a new kind of library altogether.

Through the twelfth century and into the Renaissance, the libraries stayed small. A twentieth-century reckoning of such libraries bears this out: in the ninth century, the library at Reichenau (a monastery on an island in Germany's Lake Constance) counted 415 volumes; Bobbio in tenth-century Italy held 666. These numbers put them among the largest European collections of their day, and the size of such libraries did not change much over the centuries: in the twelfth century, the library at Durham Cathedral numbered 546 books, while the famous monastery at Cluny held just over 500.

It's hard to say how large the typical European library was before the Renaissance, though, for the surviving body of catalogs is scant, and not very useful. As James Stuart Beddie, the historian who compiled the numbers above, points out, most medieval catalogs were

simply abbreviated lists of volumes; often they weren't even separately
bound, but only scribbled inside the covers or the margins of books
in the collection. The production of catalogs, after all, consumes precious resources; in a time when writing surfaces were costly things
produced at great labor, the devoting of energy to a peripheral instrument is unlikely. The catalogs typically list only the bound volumes
of the library, each of which might contain anywhere from two to
perhaps eight individual works. "In cases where several works are
found in one manuscript," Beddie writes, "those after the first were
allowed to go uncatalogued. The volumes are found cited by brief
titles, which are sometimes indefinite, as *liber Virgilii*, or *diversorum auc-
torum liber unus*." He notes, "[I]n the case of larger collections something must also be deducted to allow for duplicates, of which the
catalogues of the larger libraries show a considerable number. Thus
Cluny possessed nearly a dozen copies of Boethius's *De consolatione
philosophiae*." Augustine's works made up the bulk of the typical
medieval library—after the Bible, of course. Indeed, "the regard
which the medieval cataloguers held for Augustine is shown by the
fact that he is generally accorded first place in their lists after the
Bible." The preponderance of Augustine's books—*De civitate Dei* was
most popular—in medieval libraries strikes the modern reader as
fairly preposterous: Beddie observes that "the library of Lorsch in the
tenth century had 98 volumes of Augustine out of a total of 590, Bec
in the twelfth century had 36 volumes of Augustine, and the
monastery of St. Maurice at Naumburg at the same period had 98
manuscripts of Augustine out of 184 in the Library." These numbers
suggest that large libraries served as repositories of exemplars to be
lent for copying by smaller libraries. Perhaps it shows, too, that monks
were assigned to copy works for their own instruction as well as to
increase library collections; after the Bible, the works of Boethius and
Augustine were the staples of medieval reading.

But even in these centuries running up to the Renaissance, libraries were changing. In the cities of Europe, the university had emerged, modeled on the houses of wisdom found in the Muslim world. And it was the universities that were Nicholas's main inspiration—and his chief competition as well. Their libraries grew as rapidly as did the curiosity of their faculties. The library of the Sorbonne in Paris, which expanded dramatically in the twelfth century, exemplifies the changes universities brought to the world of the European library. Its catalog has been studied extensively by the husband-and-wife scholarly team of Richard and Mary Rouse, who affirm that rapid growth in the number of codices marked a qualitative as well as quantitative change in the nature of the library. Through the mid-thirteenth century, in fact, the books of the college weren't even organized into a true library; they were instead apportioned out among the masters of the college, who used them for their own scholarship. Only when a master traveled did the books he used get stored in common chests. But through the latter decades of the century, bequests large and small—from 4 books to 300—nearly doubled the number of books in the college. By 1290, the library contained 1,017 books. This near-doubling of the library required that it be organized; the Sorbonne's first general catalog is noted as written in 1290.

To bring order to the books, the keepers of the library at the Sorbonne used a novel tool: the alphabet. Rouse and Rouse write that "the Middle Ages did not care much for alphabetical order, because they were committed to rational order." To the medieval mind, "the universe [is] a harmonious whole, whose parts are related to one another. It was the responsibility of the author or scholar to discern these rational relationships—of hierarchy, or of chronology, or of similarities and differences, and so forth—and to reflect them in his writing." The development of this analytical approach to the written word was accompanied by the emergence in Europe of another tool: the system of Arabic numerals. In the mid-thirteenth century, scholars at Oxford first used the numbers with which they enumerated lines in manuscripts. The Rouses write that "while historians of science may wax regretful that the West was so tardy in accepting the 'radically new [Arabic] arithmetic' with its revolutionary concept of zero, we can observe to the contrary that index-makers, indifferent to the ramifications of the arithmetic, adopted the numerals eagerly, for the down-to-earth reason that these provided an unmatched means of keeping one's place." So Arabic numerals, devised and adapted in a Muslim library in eighth-century Baghdad, find their first home in Europe in the libraries of universities like Oxford.

These are the libraries disparaged by later humanists such as Valla and Petrarch, who often complained that one rare manuscript or another had languished in a medieval collection, unread and moldering away. Perhaps it can be said that in the Renaissance a medieval veneration of the text as it appeared to the reader gave way to a humanist skepticism, a wondering about the origin and travails of the book in hand. Anthony Grafton in the book *Rome Reborn* points out that "Renaissance intellectuals understood that an individual book—especially a manuscript book—can often be a historical as well as a literary document." Grafton goes on,

> In the later Middle Ages scholars had concentrated on a limited selection of the surviving texts—above all those relevant to the lectures and debates of the university curriculum. . . . The collectors and scholars of the Renaissance set out to renew and enlarge the canon. They ransacked private and institutional libraries across Europe, searching in monasteries above all for rare texts that had been copied and studied in antiquity and the early Middle Ages

but had fallen out of fashion in the era of scholasticism. . . . The Vatican became a center of this new style of scholarship: several popes, above all Nicholas V, supported the buccaneering book-hunters of the early fifteenth century, who stole whatever they could not copy *in situ*. . . .

Through these swashbuckling attempts to create a new kind of library, one of the models remained the libraries of the universities, which scholars had assiduously sought to enlarge and systematize through the thirteenth and fourteenth centuries.

With Vespasiano whispering in his ear, Nicholas now under-wrote the acquisition of a collection that reflected a new apprecia-tion for the lives books lead. He died before the collection program he instituted had made much progress. But his successor, Sixtus IV, continued and enlarged the program of the Vatican Library, provid-ing it with its first building. He also appointed the first three *scrip-tores*, each of whom was to be a specialist in one of the three ancient languages of the greatest literary, historical, and ecclesiastical impor-tance: Greek, Latin, and Hebrew. The post of *scriptore* exists to this day; its incumbents are the catalogers of the Vatican Library's collec-tions, and its chief administrative officers as well.

The catalogs those *scriptores* compiled became the key instru-ments of the new scholarship. They created detailed lists of holdings in the language for which they were responsible, which were coor-dinated to form a complete alphabetical listing of the books. The method was cumbersome; additions to the collections had to be noted marginally, or in a separate list at the end of a section. But the detail proved crucial to the scholars of humanism.

The catalog compiled in 1475 by the library's "custodians," Parmenio and Mammacino, is especially illuminating today, for it gives a picture not only of what books the library owned but of how it organized them as well. Evidently, a row of tables ran up each side of the first room of the library; to these tables books were chained by subject in great numbers. The catalog follows the layout of the tables: the first table on the left holds books of the Bible; the next table is reserved for the Fathers of the church; the following tables pass through the Doctors of the church to the works of saints and to canon law and contemporary theological works. There is a definite hierarchy here, which is mirrored across the room. According to the catalog, the table facing the biblical books contains philosophy: Aristotle with his commentators Averroës and Avicenna, Plato, and Hermes Trismegistus; the next table, facing Jerome and Augustine on the sacred side, holds astrology and mathematics; the Doctors of the church find their secular counterparts in the poets, including Ovid and Virgil; canon law finds its counterpart in rhetoric and oratory; and so on through the first room of the library. The next room, as documented in the catalog, contains tables filled with works in Greek organized in the same fashion. Though this scheme differs in its particulars, it is reminiscent of the bicameral epistemology of Cassiodorus's *Institutiones*, with the realms of the sacred and the secular reflecting and completing each other. As humanism sought to recapture the sublimities of ancient Latin, on the one hand, and to authenticate Scriptures—and the power of the church—on the other, its libraries recapitulated the symmetries of classical antiquity. It isn't clear how the books were kept on their tables, though in the catalog their titles are listed in alphabetical order within each subject area. Thus the library and its catalog reflect that, as late as the fifteenth century, the rational order of knowledge and the arbitrary order of the alphabet were locked in an uneasy truce. By the eighteenth century, however, continued growth in the collections had made the old catalog useless; and the new one brought the triumph of the arbitrary: this catalog was entirely alphabetical, without the rational fiction of division by subject.

The scholarship made possible by such a comprehensive symmetry did not always benefit the church. Lorenzo Valla used the new kind of scholarship fostered by the library to show that the Donation of Constantine—a document that allegedly showed that the first Christian emperor had given Rome to the church—was a fraud and forgery. The Donation of Constantine, however, was the foundation of papal claims to authority over Rome. In the sixteenth century, the librarian Girolamo Sirleto would place Valla's attack on the Donation of Constantine on the list of prohibited books he drew up for the Holy Office; such works as the histories of Zosimus—"the pagan who had had the bad taste to blame the fall of Rome on Christianity," in Anthony Grafton's arch description—he hid, according to a frustrated French reader, in the "deepest and most obscure part of the Vatican library." In the Counter-Reformation, Sirleto discovered what librarians have long known: that the best place to hide books, often, is the library. But Sirleto was not content merely to secrete away unwanted books; he burned them, too, putting the torch to a set of Byzantine texts denouncing the Roman church.

Michel de Montaigne, who visited the library during Sirleto's time, was able to circumvent politics. "I saw the library without any difficulty," he writes;

anyone can see it thus, and can make whatever extracts he wants; and it is open almost every morning. I was guided all through it and invited by a gentleman to use it whenever I wanted. Our ambassador was leaving Rome at that time without having seen it, and complained that they wanted him to pay court to Cardinal Sirleto, master of this library, for this permission [to see the library]: and, he said, he had never been able to see that handwritten Seneca, as he hugely desired to do. Fortune brought me to it, since on this testimony of his I considered the thing hopeless. Opportunity and opportuneness have their privileges, and often confer to the common people what they refuse to kings. Curiosity often gets in its own way, as also do greatness and power.

Such machinations are well in the past for the Vatican Library, however. Today, it is one of the most delightful scholarly libraries in the world. To use it, scholars must file through the gate past the young Swiss Guards with their knickers and their many languages, then take the long walk deep into the Città Vaticana, along the cobbled roads in the shadow of massive walls and arches as the cacophony of Rome's ubiquitous traffic gradually recedes. The bustle and hum of contented scholars fills broad, sunlit reading rooms, while the cheery staff answer questions and fill requests, patiently waiting for their polyglot patrons to put their needs into comprehensible Italian. Here and there sit monks in their cassocks and nuns in their habits, their faces bathed in the glow of laptop screens. Across the courtyard outside, a small café built into the ruins of a massive Renaissance fountain provides readers with good espresso, pastries, and free *panini* in the afternoons, which readers eat standing as they chatter away with librarians and students. Throughout the library, there is an energy and a joy that, in too many other rare books and manuscripts libraries, almost always remains suppressed. But it's there, like the books Sirleto tried, but ultimately failed, to hide in the gloomy stacks.

CHAPTER FOUR

The Battle of the Books

The number of books grew dramatically from the fifteenth century to the sixteenth, engendering a mixture of excitement and anxiety that was by no means limited to the Vatican. The humanist fascination with antiquity had developed from the subversive fancy of academics into an influential tool of authority. As science threatened the supremacy of theology and its legitimating influence in the political sphere, rulers sought the preservation of their power in classical ideals. In this sense, the library, which felt the pangs of change as books increased in number and kind, became a battleground of contesting ideologies. Was it a storehouse of wisdom, preserving timeless ideals for the edification of those burdened with rulership? Or could it become a garden of books, in which knowledge proliferated and flourished in limitless colors and forms?

Harvard College sprang up in the midst of these debates; in

fact, the college began its life as a library. John Harvard, the Puritan minister who endowed the school, had earned his M.A. at Emmanuel College, Cambridge, in 1635 before moving to Massachusetts, where he ministered to the congregation at Charlestown. He died just three years later, leaving his estate to the new school established for preachers up the road in the village of Newtowne. The core of his gift was a library of 260 titles, some 400 volumes in all. Harvard's collection reflected his Puritan beliefs; about three-quarters of his books were works of theology, most of them biblical commentary and collections of Puritan sermons. Cicero, Seneca, and Homer figured among the classical choices, but aside from these there were no literary works; this was the collection of a working Puritan minister in a hardscrabble colony in the New World. But the books legitimized the little school, provided it with the firm intellectual foundation a college needed. The school was grateful, taking its late benefactor's name, and Newtowne renamed itself Cambridge, after the late minister's alma mater.

Harvard College was a Puritan school, born in an era when English education—like all of English society in the years preceding the Glorious Revolution—was divided along religious lines. During Elizabeth's reign, English intellectuals had been infected with Renaissance curiosity about all things. The guiding light of this change in English thought was Francis Bacon, who in the Tudor era had called thinkers to attend not to words but to things—to put aside the hairsplitting critical machinations of the Middle Ages in favor of observation and experimentation. His parsing of all human knowledge into three categories—memory, wisdom, and imagination—became an organizing principle of empirical thought. In his system, Bacon eschewed the division of sacred and secular, harking back to classical epistemologies that emphasized relations among disciplines of the mind. His taxonomy enjoyed a lasting influence:

Diderot adopted the scheme in volume 1 of his 1751 *Encyclopédie*, and it has been called the forerunner of modern library classifications. With most of his contemporaries, Bacon had understood thought, like all human toil, to be the product of the fall of Adam and Eve; unlike almost any thinker before him, he allowed himself to believe that that fall was reversible. And the vehicle of the reversal, the recovery of "that right over nature which belongs to [mankind] by divine bequest," was nothing less than thought and its products. "Let us hope," he wrote, "that there may spring helps to man, and a line and race of inventions that may in some degree subdue and overcome the necessities and miseries of humanity."

But after Cromwell's death and the Restoration, the intellectual complexion of England changed, and Bacon's influence became polarized. In 1664, the Dissenters, Protestants who questioned the pomp and authority of the Anglican Church, had been forced out of the universities, thus closing to them the surest routes to power and position. Dissenting ministers in turn set up their own academies, in which Puritan theology and Baconian science held sway over the classical curriculum of Cambridge and Oxford. The mixture seems an unlikely one today, in our time of battles between the sacred and the secular, between creationism and the theory of evolution. But to the seventeenth-century mind, biblical literalism and scientific empiricism were cut from the same cloth; both followed Bacon in their reliance on the authority of the evidence as it lay before one's eyes. This was in strict contrast to the more secular classical curriculum, where the authority of tradition and the salutary value of imitation and emulation were taken, as it were, on faith.

One of the pioneers of the Dissenters' Bible-and-science curriculum was Charles Morton, who had operated an academy from about 1662 (the year the Dissenters were turned out of the universities) until 1685. During that time, it ranked among the best known and most respected, counting Daniel Defoe among its proud and worldly graduates. Finally, though, life in England for a man of Morton's beliefs had grown too risky, and he moved to America, where he became vice-president of Harvard College. Strictly speaking, Harvard was not a dissenting academy—and no doubt this is what attracted Morton. It was something more: a true college, enjoying the full patronage of the colonial government. In England, too, the Puritans had made inroads into the educational establishment; John Harvard's own college, Emmanuel, had been endowed by Puritans as an instantiation of dissent within the precincts of old Cambridge. But only in the religious utopia of Massachusetts could a fully empowered Puritan school come into its own. Harvard College would be the Cambridge and the Oxford of the Puritan Commonwealth, attuned to reason and revelation as the wellsprings of its power to turn boys into men.

Through the 1600s, the library of Harvard College grew slowly and erratically, still dependent on the generosity of donors (a dependency that has not changed, except for the number of donors and their largesse). But through this growth it remained largely a theological library, consistent with the college's mission of producing ministers for the Massachusetts Bay Colony. The books of the English Puritan minister Theophilus Gale were received into the library in 1679, and these, like Harvard's, were mostly theological. And as the library fitfully grew, conditions remained rustic within it. A later donor, Thomas Hollis of London, found the state of the library intolerable. In 1725, he wrote to the college,

> Your library is reckond here to be ill managed, . . . you want seats to sett and read, and chains to your valluable books. . . . [Y]ou let your books be taken at pleasure home to Mens houses, and many are lost, your (boyish) Students take them to their chambers, and

teare out pictures & maps to adorne their Walls, such things are not good; if you want room for modern books, it is easy to remove the less usefull into a more remote place, but do not sell any, they are devoted.

Hollis tempered his criticisms with a generosity his heirs would emulate; by 1764, when on a cold night in January a fire destroyed the library, their gifts had swelled the library to some five thousand volumes, making it the largest library in British North America. By then, it reflected the whole range of learning in its Baconian scope; memory, wisdom, and imagination were all fully represented. But even a collection of books like this, universal as it may have been in scope and aspiration, was still compact enough to fit into one large room on the upper floor of Harvard Hall, shelved by size—the most efficient use of space—in perhaps as few as twenty-three bookcases.

By the time Harvard's library burned, the English intellectual scene had changed again. The science that the Dissenters had welcomed into their schools had come to dominate the universities, and even a preachers' college·on the frontiers of the growing British Empire needed a steady supply of books. Another Hollis, Thomas Hollis V, gave £500 to establish the library's first endowed book fund, and the library began its steady recovery and growth. Today, the university's online catalog—the Harvard On Line Library Information System, or HOLLIS—records a collection of over ten million books, some of which continue to be purchased with the income of Hollis's money to this day.

A CENTURY BEFORE the fire at Harvard, libraries in general were still quite modest in size, scope, and aspiration. Those few dissenting academies that had libraries at all would have had collections much like Harvard's, which contained sermons, the works of the church Fathers, and apocalyptic tracts, along with a smattering of historical works and "philosophical" journals, in which articles of the latest scientific discoveries were to be found. And yet in its openness to criticism, and its ready acceptance of the generosity and guidance of progressive-minded donors, Harvard, like the dissenting academies, was ready to receive into its library the works of modern writers. Librarians at Oxford and Cambridge, on the other hand, had little interest in such nonsense. This is not to say that the university libraries did not collect and make available the products of a flourishing scientific book trade, which flowed chiefly from the pens of college fellows. But even though it was possible to learn about science at the universities, and possible also to read widely and well, the barriers to a "modern" education were formidable among the spires, cells, and alcoves of Oxford and Cambridge. The colleges concerned themselves not with producing new scientists, engineers, and artists but with turning young gentlemen into statesmen and leaders in the Anglican Church. For all their notoriety, even the great university scientists like Isaac Newton and Robert Boyle had little influence over the undergraduate curriculum. College students being groomed for the church or positions of secular authority were not systematically exposed to "natural philosophy," either in formal classes or in private tuition. And without classes to provide an introduction to the library's books on science, most students had no idea they existed.

The curriculum deemed necessary for the work of turning privileged boys into powerful men was neither theological nor scientific, but classical, and one of its finest products was the baronet Sir William Temple. A politician, famed diplomat, and classicist manqué, Temple in the 1690s retired to his Surrey estate, Moor Park. There, with the help of his young secretary—a distant cousin named Jonathan Swift—he devoted the full measure of his time to intellectual affairs, which were every bit as riven with debates, intrigues, and excursions as the European diplomacy of his earlier career. It was the end of the seventeenth century, and a new quarrel had heated up among England's intellectual elite—one that both conformed to and transcended the sectarian conflict between Puritans and Anglicans. It began over the question of progress: was it possible, or even desirable, that people should build upon the wisdom of the ancients?

Temple had followed the conflict from the start. He knew that in 1687 Charles Perrault had recited a poem before the French Academy, celebrating the convalescence of the sick Louis XIV, in which he praised the king and the age he represented, holding it up as a golden era that outdid the glories of ancient Rome. The controversy that stemmed from Perrault's recitations was acted out in a torrent of pamphlets rolling off the Parisian presses. At home, in England, Newton's theories were having their profound effect on the chattering classes, who sought to square the image of a cold and clockwork-driven universe with the notion of a creative, personal God. Temple kept himself abreast of this emerging battle of the ancients and moderns, and as he followed the debate he became dismayed. The thought that modern writers could hope to equal the heights of Homer and Pindar pained him. Temple allied himself firmly with the so-called ancients—with those who believed that the classics represented the zenith of man's achievement on earth, and that modern authors could hope to do no more than imitate, chastely and modestly, the sublime patterns of the ancient poets, historians, and dramatists. Seeing the primacy of the classics endangered both at home and abroad, Temple thrust himself into the debate, bringing it definitively to England's shores. In 1690, he published a pamphlet of his own, *Of Ancient and Modern Learning*.

In the essay, Temple argues that one of modern learning's chief problems is its reliance on books. It is not more books we need, he writes—the ancients had plenty of those; but they had learning also, and taste. And the mere proliferation of books is no guarantee of an expansion in learning and taste. Modern learning is too cloistered; the life of letters should be what it was for the Romans: at once personal and political, and vigorous above all. "The modern scholars," Temple writes, go too much "in quest of books, rather than men, for their guides, though these are living, and those, in comparison, but dead instructors; which like a hand with an inscription, can point out the straight upon the road but can neither tell you the next turnings, resolve your doubts, or answer your questions. . . ." The books one should read, he avers, are simply chosen: they are the oldest ones, those written nearest the time of the Homeric golden age. These books are not to be taken apart and examined scientifically by the nit-picking philologist but to be read reverentially, as the scripture of worldly power. As examples, Temple holds up the *Epistles* of the Greek tyrant Phalaris and the *Fables* of Aesop, two works that had long been thought to be among the earliest of classical writings.

Temple's choice of exemplars was unfortunate in more ways than one. Phalaris was an unsavory character, who earned the credentials of a tyrant by roasting his enemies alive in a brazen bull. To Temple, however, this hardly disqualified the king from a life of letters. The problem, instead, was that the *Epistles* was a forgery—composed in antiquity, yes, but much later than Phalaris's own time. This was particularly evident to a classicist named Richard Bentley, who knew that the Greek dialect Phalaris spoke was vastly different from the later Attic Greek in which the *Epistles* was composed. In a retort to Temple he published under the title *Dissertation upon the Epistles of Phalaris*, Bentley chided the diplomat for his injudicious choices and his superficial classicism.

As Bentley had attacked the rigor of Temple's classicism, so his protégé, the young scholar William Wotton, charged after the notion

central to Temple's argument and outlook: that the ancients had created mankind's greatest works in the arts and sciences, next to which
the work of modern thinkers paled. It is the modern's scientific
approach to the arts of antiquity, Wotton argues, that gives him
greater insight into the classical world. He acknowledges how
deeply this notion disturbs the gentleman scholars of Temple's stripe:

> To pore upon old MSS. to compare various Readings; to turn over
> Glossaries, and old Scholia upon Ancient Historians, Orators and
> Poets; to be minutely critical in all the little Fashions of the
> Ancient Greeks and Romans, the Memory whereof was, in a
> manner, lost within L or a C Years after they had been in use; may
> be good Arguments of a Man's Industry, and Willingness to
> drudge; but seem to signifie little to denominate him a great
> Genius, or one who was able to do considerable Things himself.

Temple decried the proliferation of text engendered by the
printing press. Wotton, too, acknowledges that the availability of vast
numbers of books has wrought a change in learning—but it is a
change, he argues, for the better. "When copies of Books, by Printing, were pretty well multiplied," he writes, "Criticism began; which
first was exercised in setting out Correct Editions of Ancient
Books." Wotton admits that such intellectual work has since become
"Fashionable Learning"; and if progress seems to have slowed, it is
not "because the Parts of Men are sunk, but because the Subject is,
in a manner exhausted." Wotton further allows that philology has
been accused of "Pedantry, because it has sometimes been pursued
by Men who seemed to value themselves upon Abundance of Quo-
tations of Greek and Latin, and a vain Ostentation of diffused Reading, without anything else in their Writings to recommend them."
He holds, however, that such difficult work will always produce a

great deal of fruitless labor and that, despite their haul of dross, the philologists have unearthed enough scholarly treaures "to commend the great Sagacity, as well as the Industry of these later Ages" when compared to antiquity.

When Temple looked at the explosion of new printed books, he saw no "Industry," but only diffusion, decay, and petty bickering. To Wotton, however, the disputes of the moderns, and the new books emerging from them, only prove the vigor and progressive potential of modernity when compared with a monolithic, centralized Roman Empire, in which "one Common Interest guided that vast Body." In letters as with everything else, all roads once led to Rome—a condition that ultimately proved stultifying; "Whereas now," Wotton observes, "every Kingdom stand[s] on its own Bottom, they are all mutually jealous of each other's Glory, and in nothing more than in Matters of Learning." The bickering that Temple despised—though he wasn't above taking part in it—Wotton denominates an element of the modern way of learning:

> Disputes, though many times very pedantically managed, and with an Heat misbecoming Learned Men, yet had this good Effect, that while some were zealous to secure the Glory of the Invention of Things already discovered, to their own Countries; others were equally solicitous to add a more undisputed Honour to them, by new Invention which they were sure no Man could possible challenge.

Wotton understood that the ancients had produced their books in a state of progressive zeal and abundant energy. To write books and dispute over them, he argues, is to truly emulate the ancients. But in Temple's view, these disputations had only encumbered the classical texts with so many glossaries, footnotes, and indices. In reducing the great works of antiquity to so much textual matter under the philological microscope, Temple felt, the moderns robbed the ancient texts of their sublime uniqueness, their untouchability. For Wotton, though, as for his mentor Richard Bentley, this new approach simply heralded the arrival of a new sensibility, in which the apparatuses of scholarship—the collations, the dissertations, the growing libraries—had in their scope a kind of sublimity as well.

In their pamphlets, Wotton and Bentley struck a blow at one of England's best-known aristocrats. Entering the field of public debate, they were as ill equipped politically as they were well prepared intellectually. Wotton, like the great French essayist Montaigne, had been raised speaking Latin as his first language; his father had paraded ten-year-old William among the salons of England like an intellectual Mozart, exhorting him to declaim in Latin and extemporize in Greek and Hebrew for astonished audiences. Wotton's later mentor was not of gentle birth; but like Cicero, Bentley had risen from affluent but common origins to the summit of the English intellectual world. Friend of Isaac Newton, Samuel Pepys, and John Evelyn, Bentley was England's most esteemed classicist. A clergyman, theologian, and public intellectual, who hardly restricted his attention to matters of classical philology, he also wrote and lectured about atheism and the theological implications of Newton's ideas on gravity. In 1694, he was made a Fellow of the new Royal Society, and appointed Keeper of the Royal Library.

At this time, the Royal Library, like the decidedly more modest library of Harvard College, was housed in a single room, this one above the kitchen in London's Palace of St. James. The state of the library, with books scattered among the shelves and on tables in no particular order, was widely deplored. The collection, like the room, was a hodgepodge; built by several monarchs and their amanuenses, it reflected a variety of motives. Whereas Henry VII had acquired fewer than two hundred volumes, mostly of a devotional nature, Henry VIII was more of a bibliophile. Not only was he an assiduous collector, but he also used his books, and many of the volumes he added to the library are filled with his marginalia. The elaborately cuffed pointing hands he sketched in them are particularly charming; on a summary page in an ecclesiastical work, a long, elegant finger stretches upward to point out the words *De peccato in spiritum sanctum* (of sin in the holy spirit). Henry VIII seemed to seek guidance and justification for his actions, political and personal, among the books of a rapidly growing library—and his library grew especially strong in the tractate literature of the Protestant Reformation, in which events he strove to play a fundamental role.

The Royal Library continued to grow with the subsequent monarchs. Elizabeth's additions are surprisingly sparse and enigmatic; they seem to consist chiefly of presentation copies and gifts, out of keeping with her reputation as a writer and talented linguist. Henry, Prince of Wales, by contrast, had a voracious appetite for scientific works, and James I made sure to collect everything written against his reign. In the eighteenth century, George III would, with the help of Samuel Johnson and others, build the Royal Library into one of the most extraordinary—and extraordinarily beautiful—collections of books in the world. It now resides in the new British Library, in a great glass tower in the center of the public concourse, from within which its many fine bindings glitter like jewels. But at the end of the seventeenth century, the library was a mishmash of classical works acquired for the edification of monarchs, church literature, and politico-theological tracts.

When Bentley assumed the role of keeper of the royal collection, he was aghast at its state. He immediately moved to secure certain funding for the library and to turn it from a moribund curiosity cabinet into an international institution of higher learning.

In so doing, he articulated a vision of the universal library that was strikingly ahead of its time. In a proposal published in broadsheet form, he laid out the problem for the reading public: "[the library] has gradually gone to great Decay, to the great dishonour of the Crown and the whole Nation. The Room is miserably out of Repair; and so little, that it will not contain the Books that belong to it . . . many valuable Manuscripts are spoiled for want of Covers." Bentley went on to complain that "above a Thousand" books waited to join the collection, but were still "unbound and useless"—this in violation of the Act of Printing, by which printers were required to deposit copies of their works in the Royal Library in order to secure copyright. This law, which dated to the Elizabethan era, had long been neglected; as a result, few of the thousands of titles printed in England throughout the seventeenth century had made their way to the Royal Library. Bentley would lobby hard for enforcement of the Act of Printing. He further proposed paying the library's way with a trust fund endowed by a tax on paper, to ensure the growth and magnificence of the library. The library that would result from these measures, he wrote, should be "so contriv'd for Capaciousness and Convenience, that every one that comes here, may have two hundred thousand volumes, ready for his use and service."

Bentley had in mind here a library unlike any other in the world at the time. Even the Vatican Library was not such an institution, for though truly vast, its collection was at this time all but unavailable for true scholarly work. Bentley's own son would later visit the Vatican Library, writing to his father with complaints about the difficulty he had in using the library, which was frequently closed for feasts and holidays. Bentley's vision for the Royal Library departs strikingly from such a model. In an important sense, it harks back to the ideal of the universal library of antiquity, of which Alexandria's libraries were the best-remembered exemplars. But in his ambitions, Bentley was forward looking, too; aspects of his grand plans anticipate the research libraries of the nineteenth and twentieth centuries. For instance, he imagined the library's becoming a center of intellectual activity, where scholarly societies might hold "Conferences . . . about matters of Learning."

> The Royal Society is a noble Instance in one Branch of Knowledge; what Advantage and Glory may accrue to the Nation, by such Assemblies not confined to one Subject, but free to all parts of good Learning. . . .
>
> The Wall that shall encompass the Library, may be cased on the insides with Marbles of ancient Inscriptions, Basso Relievo's Etc. either found in our own Kingdom, or easily and cheaply to be had from the African Coast, and Asia the Less. . . .
>
> Upon this Parliamentary Fund, the Curators, if occasion be, may take up Money at Interest, so as to lay out two or three years Revenues to buy whole Libraries at once. . . .

A copy of Bentley's proposal resides in the British Library, now installed in its new home on Euston Road in North London. It thrives in an extraordinary building, designed by the architect Sir Colin St. John Wilson, that is the happy flowering of Bentley's grand and visionary impulse. Books arrive from the bowels of the stacks, riding their own system of conveyors and escalators, emerging in vast reading rooms filled with light. Outside the reading rooms, the public takes in exhibitions that display some of the most glorious books in the world; meanwhile, "Learned Societies" meet among the "Basso Relievo's," their deliberations inspired by the traffic in texts and knowledge swirling all around them. Altogether, it looks astonishingly like the institution Bentley had hoped would replace the musty little room over the palace kitchen.

✦

IT IS IN THAT SHABBY LIBRARY OF OLD, however, that the most enduring picture of the quarrel of the ancients and moderns, as depicted by Jonathan Swift, is set. At the time of the quarrel, the young Swift was enjoying his tenure as factotum to Temple. He shared Temple's distrust of so-called progress; as his own work matured, his antipathy toward modern thinkers, especially those of the Royal Society, became a rich diet upon which to feed his satire. In 1704, he wrote a story called "A full and true account of the battel fought last Friday between the antient and the modern books in St. James's library," better known today simply as "The Battle of the Books." In it, he imagines the cramped and dusty room of books in Bentley's care as a vast field of battle—or perhaps he imagines the whole field of intellectual dispute in Europe as a library, though one far different from the inadequate collection kept at St. James. This is a library in which the books themselves are at war, not their critics or their advocates—where the books mix together, shifting in place and pattern, and contest among themselves for pride of place on the shelves. Like Bentley, Swift could well imagine the possibilities that emerged when great quantities of books were brought together; for him, as for his mentor Temple, a distinctly dystopian vision emerges, in marked distinction to the hopeful fantasies of Bentley and Wotton.

Swift's battle transcends the nooks of the library room. It begins,

OPPOSITE: *The frontispiece of the 1710 edition of Swift's "Battel of the Books," showing the melee in the library in St. James. The bee and the spider appear in the upper left. Houghton Library *EC7.Sw551T.1710. By permission of Houghton Library, Harvard University. Photograph by Stephen Sylvester and Bob Zinck, HCL imaging services.*

in fact, on the very flanks of mythical Parnassus. The moderns, having grown jealous of their predecessors' home on the summit, demand a change:

> Either that the Ancients would please to remove themselves and their effects down to the lower summity, which the Moderns would graciously surrender to them, and advance in their place; or else that the said Ancients will give leave to the Moderns to come with shovels and mattocks, and level said hill as low as they shall think it convenient.

The physical combat among the actual books, which plays out in the Royal Library at St. James, follows this initial confrontation. Swift is concerned about the role of pamphlets, those quickly authored and often poorly edited texts that were the chief medium of the quarrel of the ancients and moderns—for it is indeed these "books" in particular whose arrival in the physical library stirs controversy among the resident volumes. These ephemera he likens to the battle trophies set up by Greek heroes after battle. "These trophies," Swift writes,

> have largely inscribed on them the merits of the cause, a full impartial account of such a battle, and how the victory fell clearly to the party that set them up. They are known to the world under several names, as disputes, arguments, rejoinders, brief considerations, answers, replies, remarks, reflections, objections, confutations.

Swift further tells us that "the chiefest and largest" such trophies "are removed to certain magazines they call libraries, there to remain in a quarter purposely assigned them, and from thenceforth begin to be called Books of Controversy." These books, being "haunted by

the most disorderly spirits, have always been confined in a separate
lodge," where they are bound with "strong iron chains." This
method, which long kept peace in the libraries, is now no longer
sufficient because a new kind of book, "instinct with a most malignant spirit," has emerged in the war "between the learned about the
higher summity of Parnassus."

These "trophies" in Swift's satire have a double meaning: they
are the pamphlets in which the dispute was pursued; at the same
time, they represent the books of science, philology, and popular theology that are cluttering up the Parnassan library of old. Swift
acknowledges that such books are nothing new—except that in former times only the "chiefest and largest" of them found a place in
the library. Now these books arrive in a torrent—too quickly to be
bound, in the Royal Library's case—each one demanding its own
unique place in the library.

INCREASINGLY, it was in a new breed of pamphlets and journals
that the most important intellectual disputes took place. As the education of the gentleman had been founded strictly on classical literature, it had left out the emerging discourses of science, politics, and
economics; more and more, those topics thrived in publications like
the *Athenian Mercury*. Founded in 1691, the main organ of a group
of coffeehouse wits who called themselves the Athenian Society, its
full title was *The Athenian Gazette, or Casuistical Mercury, Resolving All
the Most Nice and Curious Questions Proposed by the Ingenious*. This
fuller title describes the effort well: the editors accepted questions
posed by readers on any and all topics, to which they sought the
most ingenious answers possible. Five to ten such questions appeared
twice weekly, the whole thing printed on a single sheet of paper not
much larger than letter size. As Gilbert McEwen shows in *The Oracle of the Coffee House*, his study of the journal, the *Mercury* was a

source of education for the "middling sort" of person—shopkeepers and tradespeople with little formal education, and the professional class emerging from the dissenting academies. Strikingly progressive, the paper consistently championed education for the working classes and for women. The range of questions the editors entertained is vast; nothing lay outside their expertise. A single issue might entertain such questions as "What sort of Government is best?"; "Why can an Owl see better by night than by Day?"; and "If it be lawful for a Man having buried his Wife, to marry her own Sister, the first leaving issue behind her?"

Despite his distaste for the vulgar curiosities that seemed to pass for modern thinking, Swift found cause for hope in the early numbers of the *Mercury*. His mentor Temple was among those who offered questions for the learned members of the Athenian Society to ponder. Evidently, he encouraged Swift to take the paper's use of the Athenian moniker seriously, and to expect that the "Society" would offer sober and learned guidance to England's burgeoning reading public. Swift's first published poem, in fact, is his "Ode to the Athenian Society," in which he extolled the "great Unknown, and far-exalted Men" whose wisdom filled both sides of the *Mercury*'s sheet twice weekly. Later Swift learned that this "Society" was actually composed of just three Grub Street hacks. Its publisher and guiding spirit, a bookseller by the name of John Dunton, was a product of the dissenting academies who flourished in the book trade of London's coffeehouse demimonde. He had even traveled to New England, where he met with Cotton Mather, visited a lecture given to Christianized Indians at Natick, and sold books at Harvard (some of which may have ended up in the library). Dunton championed precisely the new kind of book that, in Swift's estimation, was cluttering the Royal Library. Indeed, he seems never to have had an experience in life that he didn't deem fit to publish in book form.

He memorialized his New England trip in an autobiography he called *The Life and Errors of John Dunton*, which he brought out, doggedly, in some thirty editions. When his second wife's promised generous dowry failed to materialize, he initiated a pamphlet campaign against his mother-in-law.

Swift must have been chagrined to discover the flimsy nature of his beloved "Society." In fact, he later skewered Dunton, along with the decidedly more august—and authentic—Royal Society, in his *Tale of a Tub*. But although Dunton's *Mercury* was founded on a literary hoax, his writers did their best to answer questions honestly and comprehensively. They preferred in all things the evidence of experiment over the authority of ancient sources, though when one was unavailable, the other would do. In some questions, they relied on the latest empirical science. In answer to the question "What Matter is the Sun made of?" they cited the observations of contemporary astronomers; in their response to a question about the existence of centaurs and fauns, however, they referred assuredly to evidence in Plato, Thales, and Plutarch. In the quarrel of the ancients and moderns, they took no discernible side—though in their energy and their commitment to the progress of knowledge they were thoroughly modern. But overall, Temple's and Swift's relations with the *Mercury* suggest that it was less a partisan of one position in the battle than a battlefield unto itself.

Editors and readers of sheets like the *Mercury* advanced the modernity that the genteel education assiduously avoided, thereby following William Wotton's advice in emulating the energy and initiative of the ancients rather than the empty shells of their poetical forms. Above all, they were hungry to read—a hunger they sated with steady diets of the books and pamphlets offered by the likes of John Dunton.

Swift and Temple, however, considered these modern energies

incompatible with all that is true and beautiful in art. In time, Swift would embrace the means of modern publishing as he embraced his Irish identity, writing and publishing in pamphlets and journals, cementing his reputation both as a satirist and as a patriot. He would co-opt the tools of hoax and satire pioneered by the Grub Street hacks he despised and put them to the highest literary uses. But at the time of the quarrel of the ancients and moderns, Swift, like Temple, saw the flow of middling books from the bookshops of wits like Dunton as a torrent that threatened to engulf everything he believed in. As the historian Joseph Levine writes,

> [T]he battle of the books showed that Renaissance humanism . . . had become divided against itself. . . . By 1700 it was becoming necessary to choose either the one side or the other: either imitation or scholarship, either the standards of the ancients' rhetoric or the new techniques of modern criticism, either polished narrative or antiquarian compilation.

TO SWIFT, Richard Bentley was the chief exponent of such criticism and compilation; thus he became the chief target of the satire. As a character in "The Battle of the Books," Bentley had humiliated himself in the first fight on the summit of Parnassus. The librarian now tried to avenge himself by installing the ancients' enemies in all the "fairest apartments" of the library, while burying the ancients and their "advocates" to the dusky corners, and threatening that "upon the least displeasure" they will be "turned out of doors." But the keeper of the books couldn't keep his books straight—for there arose "a strange confusion of place among all the books in the library." Opinions on the cause of the confusion differed; some said that "a great heap of learned dust, which a perverse wind blew off from a shelf of Moderns into the keeper's eyes" was at fault; others offered

that Bentley had tried to "pick the worms out of the schoolmen"—
to criticize and collate the works of medieval Aristotelians—but that
the bookworms had infected him, "whereof some fell upon his
spleen, and some climbed into his head, to the great perturbation of
both." Still others opined the poor fellow had spent too much time
in the dark with his books and "had quite lost the situation of it out
of his head; and therefore, in replacing the books, he was apt to mistake and clap Des Cartes next to Aristotle; poor Plato had got
between Hobbes and the Seven Wise Masters, and Virgil was
hemmed in with Dryden on one side, and Withers on the other."

With his caricature of Bentley, Swift may have offered the first
instance of that literary cliché—the doddering librarian. Indeed, the
entire modern iconography of the library is present here, all the
stereotypes are in motion: the learned pedant, crabbed and dust-
addled, himself consumed by and consuming bookworms, is lost in
the vastness of the library. The library itself is a place of dark,
"obscure corners," full of shadows among which books and readers
alike may be lost. It is a kind of literary purgatory, in which texts of
all kinds and qualities risk confounding their individual identities. A
place of stasis, of stultifying confusion, it is also a place of (mock)
tumult, intellectual combat, and literary confabulation. Offering
sweeping panoramas and minute scenes, Swift's library becomes the
beaches and plains of Homer's Ilium—only transposed perfectly into
satire's key, in which the transports of passion, from mortal terror to
exultance, are replaced by a minor scale running from boredom and
resentment to pedantic vainglory. Swift digresses kaleidoscopically
throughout his work, focusing on one skirmish after another, always
changing his focal length.

The library of Swift's satire is the prototype of the universal
library, not only in numerical terms—for Swift imagines a library
teeming with books in far greater numbers than were typically

found in libraries of the time—but in its spirit as well: for conflict among books is what the universal library is about. The choices are not made for the reader; the reader must do the choosing, and the books must compete for his attention. In this, Swift comes much closer to the fondest hopes of his antagonist Bentley than he might have realized at the time.

DURING HIS LONG LIFE, Jonathan Swift built an admirable library of his own. In this respect, he was much like other learned gentlemen of the seventeenth and eighteenth centuries. Edward Gibbon, for example, built an enormous library for himself at Lausanne. Gibbon's library was a working library, of course—he drew on it almost exclusively during the long composition of the *Decline*—and he kept close track of its contents. In fact, he devised one of the first card catalogs, made out on the back of playing cards, to ensure quick access to all of the books. Swift's library, too, is that of a working writer, scholar, and divine. Harold Williams's work *Dean Swift's Library, with a Facsimile of the Original Sale Catalogue and Some Account of Two Manuscript Lists of His Books* gives a complete account of the state of Swift's books and their disposition at his death. The core of Williams's essay is its exploration of the extent to which Swift might have used some of the books he owned to inform his writing. He is less concerned with the notion of Swift as the author of a library. But by taking that perspective, we can, I think, discover something about the ways in which libraries are created and used.

The sale catalog contains entries for 657 volumes, a few of which are manuscripts. Of these, 73 entries were starred, meaning that those volumes contained annotations by Swift. Williams observes that in Swift's library, the number of theological works, whether in Latin or modern languages, is not larger than might be expected in a divine who, to say the least, was scarcely by taste or inclination fitted for his adopted profession. Little more than a hundred, less than a sixth of the whole, can be counted with books serving the studies of an ecclesiastic, which, if we take into account the fashion of the day, is certainly not a large proportion.

So in Swift's own library we find the irony of his satire reflected. For unlike the typical ecclesiastical library—unlike that of the Puritan John Harvard, for instance—Swift's shows a large number of works that spring from the modern learning. Indeed Swift, for all his railing against the usurpations of the moderns, compiled a library that was the fruit of those cultural changes which made the modern possible. Williams continues,

> The early fathers of the Church are represented by Epiphanius and Tertullian only, an indication that the Dean was content with borrowed books for what he learned in this part of his studies in divinity. Among mediaeval Christian writers Aquinas alone appears.... Continental theologians are represented by Calvin, and Melancthon; and French writers by Pascal, Bossuet, and by Richard Simon's *Histoire Critique du Vieux Testament*, a work supressed on its first publication in 1678.

Quite a few contemporary English theological authors are represented. But Swift may have bought these for the sake of form rather than out of interest; for as Williams notes, "[n]ot one of these . . . is, however, marked [in the sale catalog] as annotated by Swift." With a few ecclesiastical histories, these make up the whole of Swift's holdings in theology. The inventory of Swift's classical holdings, by contrast, is much larger, which is to be expected for a man of affairs. The preponderance of these works were Roman works, or Latin translations of Greek works, reflecting the tenor of the Augustan era.

Williams is right to remember that "there is frequently an element of chance in the way books are picked up"; many books in Swift's library would have been gifts. Nonetheless, Swift took great care in fashioning his library and in structuring it. He organized his library, it seems, as much to make an impression on the visitor as to aid him in finding and using the books. According to a letter he wrote to Alexander Pope in April 1729, the most prominently displayed books—those which the visitor "casts his eyes immediately upon" when he "comes into my closet"—are the thirty-one folio volumes of Grenovius and Graevius on Greek and Roman antiquities. These were the most expensive and visually impressive books in Swift's "closet"; thus they held pride of place. But they are also interesting for being archaeological works, and thus fruits of the modern. So Swift indeed expected his library to be "read" in a particular way—however differently it, like any text, might be read.

Swift's executors started a list of his books during his long last illness, and it gives a fair picture of the disposition of volumes in his study. The catalog follows the shelves from left to right around the room, through folios (the largest books, each page consisting of a full sheet of paper, the size of a modern atlas) and quartos (the size of a typical encyclopedia) to two shelves of duodecimos (one of the smallest book formats, in which the paper has been folded twelve times to fashion the page), all arranged by size. The sale catalog of Swift's books, drawn up after they had been removed from the deanery upon his death, similarly lists books by size. This is reminiscent of Harvard's library, and other contemporary catalogs as well. Even the largest libraries were still modest enough to allow librarians to keep track of all the books without resort to complex cataloging techniques. The canon was still intact; the books contained in even the most copious libraries, personal or institutional, were all part of the same generally recognized set of platonically ideal works. Even as Swift's library reflects the canonical ideal, its shelving by size serves to cut against it as well, treating the massive folios of archaeological drawings and studies as the visual centerpiece of the collection.

WHATEVER ITS DISPOSITION, this much is true: Swift's library was at the end of his life a far more compelling and well-cared-for collection than the Royal Library had been at the time of his writing "The Battle of the Books." As in his earlier explanation of Bentley's confusion ("a great heap of learned dust"), Swift makes use of the musty dilapidation of the royal collection in his satire, seizing on the image of a spider inhabiting a dirty, cobwebbed corner, a scene that in Swift's hands becomes an Aesopian fable, reenacting the whole quarrel of the ancients and moderns on an animalcular scale.

When a distracted, sun-drunk bee blunders through an open window into the spider's web, tearing its artful geometry, the spider protests. Reflecting the modern sensibility, the spider sees himself as entirely self-made and self-sufficient. He rages at the bee: "This large castle (to shew my improvements in the mathematics) is all built with my own hands, and the materials extracted altogether out of my own person." He acuses the bee of being a "vagabond without house or home, . . . born to no possession of your own, but a pair of wings and a drone-pipe." Swift even allows the bee to reflect Temple's inattention to the details of the dispute, I think, in the way he sweetly blunders into the spider's outer web, just as Temple stumbled into the quarrel over the authenticity of Aesop and Phalaris. The bee has studied his rhetoric, however, and is ready with an elegant retort:

[T]he question comes all to this—which is the nobler being of the two, that which, by a lazy contemplation of four inches round, by an overweening pride, feeding and engendering on itself, turns all into excrement and venom, produces nothing at last, but flybane and cobweb; or that which, by a universal range, with long search, much study, true judgment, and distinction of things, brings home honey and wax.

In his spider, Swift finds an archetype of scholarly folly familiar to his readers. Francis Bacon himself had proposed the spider as the totem of hypothetical (as opposed to empirical) philosophy, demanding that the cobwebs of apocalyptic thinking be struck down. Speculative thinkers of the seventeenth century, including Newton, used sophisticated mathematics to calculate the time of the Second Coming, much to the horror of Swift and other divines of orthodox persuasion. It's in this vein that the spider in "The Battle of the Books" mistakes the tremors and dilapidations of the web's fragile geometry for sure signs of the End Time. The "infinite numbers of flies" trapped in the spider's web, meanwhile, are the gullible readers of coffeehouse newspapers like the *Athenian Mercury*, in which millenarian speculations found a ready audience.

When the quarrel between the spider and the bee ends, it is Aesop—not the ancient author but the book, that is, who has escaped the binding chains of the library to join his fellow ancients in their fight—who fittingly remarks on the dispute:

Erect your schemes with as much method and skill as you please; yet if the materials be nothing but dirt, spun out of your own entrails (the guts of modern brains), the edifice will conclude at last in a cobweb, the duration of which, like that of other spiders' webs, may be imputed to their being forgotten, or neglected, or

hid in a corner. . . . As for us, the Ancients, we are content, with
the bee, to pretend nothing of our own beyond our wings and our
voice, that is to say, our flights and our language. . . . [I]nstead of
dirt and poison, we have rather chose to fill our hives with honey
and wax, thus furnishing mankind with the two noblest of things,
which are sweetness and light.

The web spun by the moderns from their own dirt and guts
inspires in Swift a disgust of celestial dimensions. This battle began
on Parnassus; now the Olympians, observing the biblioclastic fight
from their heavenly aerie, decide to get involved. Jupiter begins by
reading from the book of fate—"three large volumes in folio . . . The
clasps were of silver, double gilt, the covers of celestial turkey leather,
and the paper such as here on Earth might almost pass for vellum."
Jupiter recites the necessary outcome in the ancients' favor, and dis-
patches his servants to make it happen. A stricken Momus, patron
god of the moderns, appeals to the goddess Criticism for help. She
is a deity of terrible aspect, her "eyes turned inward as if she looked
only upon herself," who suckles a great horde of monsters at teats
projecting from her spleen, the bulk of which "increased faster than
the sucking could diminish it." When Momus reports that all is not
going well for the moderns, Criticism flies into a rage: "'Tis I," she
howls,

who give wisdom to infants and idiots; by me, children grow wiser
than their parents; by me, beaux become politicians, and schoolboys judges of philosophy; by me, sophisters debate and conclude
upon the depths of knowledge; and coffeehouse wits, instinct by
me, can correct an author's style and display his minutest errors
without understanding a syllable of his matter or his language. By
me, striplings spend their judgment as they do their estate, before

it comes into their hands. 'Tis I who have deposed wit and knowledge from their empire over poetry, and advanced myself in their stead. And shall a few upstart Ancients dare to oppose me?

On the field, meanwhile, the battle is now fully engaged. Paracelsus strikes first for the moderns, aiming at Galen. Aristotle responds with an arrow aimed at that arch-fiend Francis Bacon; missing its mark, it strikes Descartes, sending him reeling "till death, like a star of superior influence, drew him into his own vortex"— an allusion to Descartes's muddled cosmological theories. Suddenly Homer appears on a great horse, and rides among the moderns, laying low numberless poetasters. An armored Virgil next sallies forth "astride a dapple grey steed, the slowness of whose pace was an effect of the highest mettle and vigour." Every movement of the ancients is rhetorical and grandly aesthetic; every twitch of the moderns a grotesque abomination. Now an enormous foe gallops forth from the moderns' ranks with great clangs from his armor; when he raises his visor to parley, it is none other than Dryden. He is far too small for his armor, however, and can barely be seen within. He asks for peace with Virgil and an exchange of armor, to which the ancient agrees. "However, this glittering armour became the Modern yet worse than his own," for he finds himself too small for it. "Then they agreed to exchange horses; but when it came to the trial, Dryden was afraid and utterly unable to mount."

Swift brings the hated Bentley onto the field at last. "[I]n person the most deformed of all the Moderns; . . . His armour was patched up of a thousand incoherent pieces," as was the real Bentley's scholarship, according to his critics. Armed with a flail in one hand and a pot of shit in the other, he finds himself much disparaged by the generals. Undeterred, he sallies forth with his beloved hero, the young Wotton; together they go creeping about behind enemy lines, hoping to catch some wounded ancient unawares. Bentley finds Phalaris and Aesop asleep and steals up to finish them off; the heroes turn in their sleep, and startle him. He contents himself by stealing their armor.

Bentley next tries to drink from the spring Helicon—watering place of the Muses—but Apollo intercedes, allowing only mud to reach his lips. At the fountain, however, Wotton spies two heroes. One he doesn't recognize (this anonymous hero must be Swift himself); the second is none other than Temple, who is drinking from the fountain in great gulps. Wotton tries to deal him a blow from behind, but—because of the bungling intercession of his mother, Criticism, and patron, Momus—he misses, and is pursued by Temple's own hero, the younger Boyle. With the aid of Athena, he transfixes both Bentley and Wotton on the point of his lance.

OF COURSE, the quarrel of the ancients and the moderns was not resolved so decisively as in "The Battle of the Books." But Swift's tale does provide "a true Account"—that of the figures that will stand for enthusiasms and anxieties about the library for generations to come. The image of the ancients as a band of brothers back-to-back at a bibliographical Agincourt, the advent of print as a flood or torrent, the doddering pedantry of the bookworm, and the hubris of the critic—these tropes are put to use in later times. A signal example is found in "The Mutability of Literature," a short narrative included in Washington Irving's *Sketch Book*, written nearly a century later. The Swiftian anxieties are still alive and well as Irving's narrator recounts a visit to an English library, where he discovers a very old, very angry book—a veteran, perhaps, from Swift's campaign—living out a miserable retirement.

The story opens with Irving in the guise of the weary traveler, who in the midst of a visit to a busy Westminster Abbey finds himself in need of peace and quiet. To escape from the schoolboys who have the run of the place, he asks the verger to admit him to the library. Their trip through the shadows is a reduced version of the descent into the underworld, or the passage back into the womb. "He conducted me through a portal rich with the crumbling sculpture of former ages," Irving writes, down a "gloomy passage," a double-locked door, up a "dark narrow staircase," which leads finally to the library. It's curious how Irving marries down to up, *purgatorio* to *paradiso*—for despite the up staircase they must climb, the library itself seems interred in the depths, among the crypts. "Buried deep within the walls of the abbey, and shut up from the tumult of the world," Irving finds himself caught in a liminal world of ancient, undisturbed books. Choosing a vellum-bound volume from the shelves, he collapses into reverie, reflecting on the works entombed here as in a catacomb, "left to moulder and blacken in dusty oblivion."

> While I sat half murmuring half meditating these unprofitable speculations with my head resting on my hand, I was thrumming the other hand upon the quarto, until I accidentally loosened the clasps; when, to my astonishment, the little book gave two or three yawns, like one awakening from a deep sleep; then a dusky hem; and at length began to talk.

The little volume is a delightful character, and Irving makes the most of it. "At first its voice was very hoarse and broken," he recounts, "being much troubled by a cobweb which some studious spider had woven across it"—a cameo appearance, perhaps, of Swift's overindustrious arachnid. Soon the book manages to clear its throat and proves "an exceedingly fluent conversable little tome."

Irving and the book discuss the life of literature, the changes language undergoes, and the fickle nature of literary fame. The little volume has been shut up entirely too long and rails dispeptically, "[W]hat do they mean by keeping several thousand volumes of us shut up here, and watched by a set of old vergers, like so many beauties in a harem, merely to be looked at now and then by the dean?" Irving tries to soothe him.

> You are not aware of how much better off you are than most books of your generation. . . . [V]ery few of your contemporaries can be at present in existence; and those few owe their longevity to being immured like yourself in old libraries; which, suffer me to add, instead of likening to harems, you might more properly and gratefully compare to those infirmaries attached to religious establishments for the benefit of the old and decrepit.

However, Irving laments, not even the library can save its books from the obscurity of the passage of time. "[W]hen I contemplate a modern library," he tells the little book,

> filled with new works, in all the bravery of rich gilding and binding, I feel disposed to sit down and weep; like the good Xerxes, when he surveyed his army, pranked out in the splendor of military array, and reflected that in one hundred years not one of them would be in existence!

Just so were Swift's ancients "pranked out" in tragic splendor. *Après ça, le déluge*—and we have in this keening a recognition of the perishability of books as objects, which always threatens to triumph over the immortality of the book as ideal. From here, Irving moves on to a dilation of the troubles of the modern library, in terms Swift would have found congenial. He notes that formerly books were rare enough to remain truly precious; men treasured and protected them for all the difficulty they went through in making and obtaining them. "But the inventions of paper and the press have put an end to all these restraints," Irving observes, and "the consequences are alarming."

> The stream of literature has expanded into a torrent—augmented into a river—expanded into a sea. A few centuries since, five or six manuscripts consituted a great library; but what would you say to libraries such as actually exist, containing three or four hundred thousand volumes; legions of authors at the same time busy; and the press going on with fearfully increasing activity, to double and quadruple the number? . . . [T]he world will inevitably be overstocked with good books. It will soon be the employment of a lifetime merely to learn their names. Many a man of passable information, at the present day, reads scarcely anything but reviews; and before long a man of erudition will be little better than a mere walking catalogue.

But the little book finds Irving's histrionics too much to bear. "'My very good sir,' said the little quarto, yawning most drearily in my face, 'excuse my interrupting you, but I perceive you are rather given to prose.'"

SWIFT TOO WAS "GIVEN TO PROSE." In his prescient imagination, however, the figure of the universal library rose prematurely into view; before Swift could satirize it, he had to invent it. The libraries caught up quickly, though. Those tens of thousands of upstart modern troops soon found their places alongside the ancients on the shelves, where they were joined inexorably by an immigrant tide from the ever-busy presses. The wrack and ruin of the library-as-battlefield drowned in the rising tide of the universal library. Swift in his vast humor prefigured the anxiety that Matthew Arnold would express in his 1885 poem "Dover Beach," in which we are stranded "as on a darkling plain / Swept with confused alarms of struggle and flight / Where ignorant armies clash by night." The bright "Sea of Faith" has finally disappeared from that plain, Arnold writes earlier in the poem, with a "long, melancholy, withdrawing roar." Parnassus, however, is always reappearing as an island newly reborn, an Avalon or an Atlantis forever discernible in the mists.

Richard Bentley, for his part, continued to run into problems with libraries. Long after the quarrel of the ancients and moderns had fizzled, he installed a young cousin, Thomas Bentley, as keeper of the library of Cambridge's Trinity College. At Richard's urging, the young librarian followed the path of a professional, pursuing a doctoral degree and taking long trips to the Continent in search of new books for the library. The college officers, however, did not approve of his activities. The library had been endowed by Sir Edward Stanhope, whose own ideas about librarianship were decidedly more modest than those of the Bentleys. In 1728, a move was made to remove the younger Bentley, on the ground that his long absence, studying and acquiring books in Rome and elsewhere, among other things, disqualified him from the post.

In his characteristically bullish fashion, Richard Bentley rode to his nephew's defense. In a letter, he admits that "the keeper [has not] observed all the conditions expressed in Sir Edward Stanhope's will," which had imposed a strict definition of the role of librarian. Bentley enumerates Sir Edward's stipulations, thereby illuminating the sorry state of librarianship in the eighteenth century. The librarian is not to teach or hold office in the college; he shall not be absent from his appointed place in the library more than forty days out of the year; he cannot hold a degree above that of master of arts; he is to watch each library reader, and never let one out of his sight ("A slavery," Bentley writes, "not to be borne by a Master of Arts now-a-days"); he is, finally, not permitted a private residence, but must allow a scholar or student to be lodged with him. Bentley concludes by offering, "Your Grace will perceive by these orders, that Sir Edward had in his view a very low notion of His Librarian."

In encouraging his young cousin to act not as a functionary but as a scholar and a professional, Bentley was once more articulating a library vision strikingly out of step with his time. He firmly felt that the work of finding, keeping, and organizing a scholarly collection of books was essential to modern scholarship, and that the keeping of libraries should be entrusted to people whose intellectual development was strong and unhindered. The dominant opinion, however, was different. Sir Edward Stanhope, whose generosity had endowed Trinity with a fine library, evidently felt that his books required nothing more than a custodian. His rules stood; the committee chastised Bentley and forced his young cousin Thomas out of office. The Bentleys' vision for the library would be affirmed, if fitfully and uncertainly, in years to come.

CHAPTER FIVE

Books for All

It was to be the year of his triumph, and yet for Enoch Soames 1891 proved more dreadful than ever. His new work unpublished, his first books out of print, Enoch peered out through an absinthe haze at a London reeling with backstabbers, tin ears, and nincompoops. Sensible of his friends' dismissal of his work and his person, he had arrived at the inescapable conclusion that the present world held no more charm for him. His hopes lay in the future: there, he was sure, his name would loom as one of the nineteenth century's poetic prophets, rightfully eclipsing the meager lights of contemporary poseurs. In his hunger for this future, finally, he made a desperate pact, a deal with the devil: an eternity in hell for the opportunity to visit the Round Reading Room of the British Library one hundred years later, to find his books in the collection, his name draped in laurels. To seal the contract, he invited the devil himself to lunch at a London café, and brought along a witness—his last friend, a newspaper writer and essayist named Max.

The journalist jumped to his friend's defense. But before he could argue the case with the devil himself (less a horned imp than an oiled and weary flâneur), his friend Soames disappeared without so much as a whiff of brimstone. The journalist awaited his friend's return, dreading the results of his expedition into the future. When Soames at last reappeared, dismayed and demoralized, the journalist knew the truth before it was uttered: Soames had failed to find his name among the authors listed in the 1991 edition of the *Catalogue of the British Library*. Worse still, in desperation, Soames had asked the library assistant for a copy of a good book on English literature of the nineteenth century. He managed to find his name in the index—a momentary pleasure—only to discover upon turning to the page that he was listed as a minor character in a short story written by his friend the journalist! Chagrined, the writer comforted his friend, but only for a short while—in a flash the devil sidled up to the café table to claim Soames's soul.

So goes the sorry tale of Enoch Soames as told by Max Beerbohm in *Seven Men*, his collection of short stories. Beerbohm wrote the story early in the twentieth century, and his imagined British Library of the future is little changed from the one he knew himself. The people all look identical, of course—after all, this is the future; they are hairless, dress in tasteful gray serge uniforms, and write a horrid, phonetically simplified version of English—but the library itself is still the nineteenth-century Round Reading Room, the volumes of the printed catalog standing sentry in their ordered ranks around the great desk at the room's navel. In Beerbohm's future library, readers still flop those cumbrous volumes on the top of their shelves with a resounding boom, still look up the texts they want among the endless pages of the catalog, still fill out little slips and sit at heated desks to await the delivery of their books. For all its wit and invention, Beerbohm's story is decidedly conservative when it comes to the need for—and even the possibility of—change in the library.

What's striking now is that Beerbohm was very nearly right: in 1991, readers still perused the many volumes of the printed catalog, still filled out their call slips in longhand. Outwardly, the library changed little between the turn of the twentieth century and the day Beerbohm's fictional poet paid his visit in 1991. All the changes—all the *future*—would seem to have taken place in the decade after 1991. Much changed at the British Library, to be sure: it moved from its British Museum quarters to a vast new complex on Euston Road; its online catalog, like those of libraries great and small around the world, fundamentally altered the way readers get and use books. But for all the changes and despite its democratization, the library remains a numinous place. As much to us as to Soames, inclusion in the library still represents a landmark in a literary life.

Inwardly, libraries in 1891 had changed a great deal over the course of the nineteenth century, in ways that made Soames's hopes quixotic. For the library had filled up; by the end of the nineteenth century, it was stocked so full of books that it had become easy to think that everyone might find a book of his or her own within its stacks. In the preceding century, Jonathan Swift could still imagine the library as a stage populated by a small number of dramatis personae whose names chimed with significance; the library then was a kind of monastery in which a few elite texts paced the hours, shook their censers, and sang in plainchant the conversation of the ages. But in the nineteenth century, the sheer proliferation of books in number and kind transformed the library from temple to market, from canon to cornucopia. That makes Soames's quest all the more tragic—for the library in which he could find no trace of himself was a model of the society it served. His absence from the library is less about literary failure in the traditional sense than about the loss of individual identity in an increasingly complex metropolitan world.

Like Enoch Soames, librarians in the nineteenth century looked to the future to fix their identity. Previously, the librarian had been animated by his relationship with books—relatively small numbers of books, organized into canons, consumed in the main by readers already intimate with them. The librarian's role, then, was largely custodial; he counted books, fetched them, and later returned them to the shelves. But with the efflorescence of printed matter and its increased consumption by a reading public, the librarian's relation with readers began to supplant his connection with the books in his charge. The principal image of the librarian switched from custodian to caregiver. In the nineteenth century, both the professional literature and the popular press presented images of librarians toiling to shape the tastes of their patrons, to conduct them through the pitfalls of the cheap, the tawdry, and the "highly seasoned" reading found in novels and newspapers toward a redeeming vision of high literary culture.

These images of the librarian bring to mind Prometheus, the Titan who presented mankind with the gift of fire. Two things are worth remembering about Prometheus: first, that he is moved by one emotion, pity, and his gift ultimately inspires another emotion, hubris, in the hearts of human beings. The tragic flaws of the Promethean impulse, pity and hubris, are the emotional poles of the librarian in the nineteenth century as well: pity for the low station of the reader, and hubris for the possibilities the library offers for the reformation of culture and society. The second thing to remember about the myth is the punishment of Prometheus. For his transgression against the power of the gods, Zeus chains the Titan to a wave-battered rock by the sea and sends down vultures to eat his immortal liver forever.

Like the Titans when Zeus and his fellow gods appeared, librarians found themselves in a ruptured universe, one with new forces in play. As the number of books grew, the intellectual integument that bound them into a cultural whole called "literature" was stretched to the breaking point. One of the mottoes of the public library movement that swept western Europe and America in the nineteenth century went like this: "a book for every person." But the search for that personal story had been an existential dilemma long before it became an issue in library science. Beerbohm knew this. He knew, too, what those uniformed readers were doing in the library when they were disturbed that summer day in 1991 by the appearance of a wild-haired, fin-de-siècle poet in their midst. They, as much as poor Enoch, were searching for themselves.

WHEN THE BRITISH MUSEUM OPENED IN 1753, few Britons would have thought to go looking for their own personal book within it. Had they tried, most would have been disappointed: though intended as Britain's national collection, it was modest by the standards of other such libraries across Europe. At its opening, it contained some 51,000 books; by the end of the eighteenth century, the number had actually declined, to approximately 48,000. This was because the museum library housed much duplicate material, which librarians assiduously sold off or gave away as practicably as they could. Then as now, book collecting was fashionable, and fashionable people tend to buy the same fashionable books. The new library depended on such genteel collections—given or purchased with the museum's meager funds—to build its own store of books. The first collection the museum purchased came from the Royal Society president Sir Hans Sloane, bought for the princely sum of twenty thousand pounds (nearly two million at today's rate). The library tried to recover from this impoverishing acquisition by sponsoring a lottery; but allegations of corruption brought the lottery to an inconclusive close, and the library was forced to rely on parliamentary whims to keep itself in operation.

The British Library also grew as a result of its role as copyright registrar, which meant that a copy of every book published in Britain had a place in its stacks. The Royal Library had played this role long before, although publishers had deposited their work only sporadically, as Richard Bentley lamented in the late seventeenth century. One hundred years later, however, Britain was both drawing inward in its sense of difference from the other nations of Europe and expanding in hopes and power as an empire—and the need to define the national literature was felt more acutely. France, too, had its copyright library—the formidable Bibliothèque Nationale, whose collections at the end of the eighteenth century had swollen to more than 300,000 books, thanks to the seizure of the libraries of aristocrats and clergy in the wake of the revolution of 1793. As the nineteenth century wore on, the British Library would catch up with, but never surpass, its French counterpart; the Continental elegance of the Bibliothèque Nationale's soaring, iron-laced vaults would provide counterpoint to the classical austerity of the Round Reading Room.

But in the first few decades of the nineteenth century Britain's national library began to grow—and in fact to balloon: by 1833, it owned nearly a quarter of a million books, a fivefold increase. Already in 1811, the *Times* of London was produced on steam-driven, drum-fed presses, and by the 1820s the use of steam to power printing presses was commonplace, and a number of technologies now converged to dramatically accelerate the pace at which books

*The old reading room of the Bibliothèque Nationale, designed by Henri Labrouste
and built in 1862. Its latticed domes and soaring columns express the sublime
power of nineteenth-century iron construction. This image appears in Diane Asséo
Griliches's book of her library photographs,* Library: The Drama Within
(Washington, D.C.: Library of Congress, 1996).

©1996 Diane Asséo Griliches

and other printed materials were produced. Printing, which had
changed little between the fifteenth and the eighteenth centuries, at
once ceased to be an artisanal craft, and the book became subject to
the mass production that was a hallmark of the industrial revolution.

One of the most fascinating images of the mass production of
books in the nineteenth century appears in the Harper Brothers
Story Book Series, which conveyed all manner of useful information to its mostly young readers. In Jacob Abbott's *The Harper Establishment; or, How the Story Books Are Made* (1855), the series examined
the machinery of its own production. Abbott gives the reader a tour
of Harper Brothers' great plant on Cliff Street and Franklin Square

in New York City, a plant that by this time was producing books "by the hundreds of thousands."

Central to Abbott's book is an engraving that depicts the idealized efficiency, coordination, and mechanization of the printing process at midcentury. Although Abbott focused on the magic of the machine—the piping of steam, the transmission of power by shafts and belts, and the glamorous dance of the presses—his grand plan of the Cliff Street building shows that at midcentury it was above all the massing of labor power, of *people*—people segregated by gender and task and regulated by that cyclopean manifestation of modernity, the clock on the wall—that turned the book from being an objet d'art to being an interchangeable part.

Abbott's series of vignettes is framed by the interlaced iron beams that make up the floors: wrought iron has—in theory, at least—emancipated the workers from the fear of fire. It allows them to use gas lighting and to operate high-temperature equipment safely, freeing production from the strictures of natural light, which formerly limited printing to small-scale production carried on in the daylight hours.

As Walter Benjamin writes in his *Arcades Project*, the nineteenth century began with the use of cast iron to frame luxury spaces like London's Crystal Palace. The Bibliothèque Nationale in Paris, too, showed off its iron skeleton, which bore the great vaults of the reading room skyward. The same iron-framing practices later transformed the stacks of the great libraries, too, allowing them to hold more books, better organized and safer from fire, than could have been imagined in the decades before. The importance of iron to nineteenth-century architecture is so great that Abbott digresses for a full chapter to explain the manufacture of iron beams and their use in construction.

In the image of the Harper Brothers plant, stages in the print-

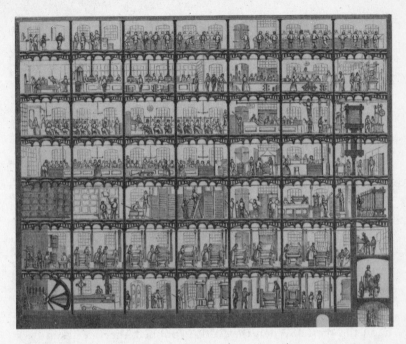

Diagram of the Harper Brothers printing plant from Jacob Abbott's The Harper
Establishment *(1855). Houghton Library B 5940.10*. By permission of
Houghton Library, Harvard University.*

ing process are framed by a web of iron beams—more pedestrian
than the soaring iron vaults of the Bibliothèque Nationale, but no
less miraculous. The room with the great wheel in the picture's
lower left-hand corner contains "the engine and machinery which
supply moving power for all the operation of the establishment,"
which is "conveyed to the different floors by a system of axles, pul-
leys, and bands." Elsewhere on this first level, hydraulic presses flat-
ten and smooth paper, and workers moisten pages to receive the ink.

At the far right, a door leads to the vaults where the printing
plates are stored. These plates were electrotypes, created by electrify-

ing blocks of hand-set type to mold a layer of copper to their surfaces. Underneath the arched entryway—where a driver is arriving,
perhaps delivering a fresh load of paper—two men illuminate a
room of the vaults with their lantern. The vault is a kind of library
where the plates, nascent books themselves, rest like jars of embryos
in a mad scientist's laboratory.

Abbott tells us that "the accumulation of electrotype plates" is
"very great"—that the stores of the "Magazine alone are rapidly
approaching ten thousand" and that "[t]here is one plate for every
page of every one of the many hundreds of volumes which the
house publishes, making from fifty to seventy tons in all." Elsewhere
he allows that this inventory increases by two hundred plates per day.
But Abbott has no use for metaphysical speculations on these masses
of type. He's content to report, "When a new edition of any book
is required, the plates are brought out from these vaults and put
upon the presses. When the work is finished, they are taken back
again to the vaults."

The building's next level contains "the great press room."
Abbott remarks that the presses weigh two tons each, making their
arrangement with respect to the columns and floor supports crucial.
Above the presses runs a series of belts connected by a shaft, which
transmits power to each press from the steam engine in the bowels
of the building. Abbott then describes the flurry of activity that goes
on in the press room:

> We observe that each of the presses is attended by a girl . . .
> [whose] duty is to *feed* the press with paper, placing one sheet at a
> time. The sheet is thrown over when it is printed by what is called
> the fly, which is a light wooden frame, like a hand with a multi-
> tude of slender fingers, which lifts the sheet when it has received
> the impression, and throws it over upon the pile formed by those

which had been printed before. At the right-hand end of the room this fly may be seen very distinctly in the act of going back after another sheet of paper, and on the other presses along the line we see it in various positions, bringing the printed sheet over.

Despite their monstrous bulk, these machines can swiftly turn out pages with their delicate mechanical fingers. "Visitors," Abbott reports, "are always particularly pleased with the life-like actions of the iron fingers" of the presses. "There is something imposing and almost sublime," he opines, "in the calm and steady dignity with which the ponderous engines continue their ceaseless toil."

Elsewhere throughout the building, books are stacked, sewn, ground, and pressed into being (especially pressed—Abbot informs his readers that no fewer than twenty-five separate machines are used to smash the books into their compact, shelf-ready shape). The top floor contains the composing room, where typesetters fill their composing sticks with type sorts, reading backward. This operation, the heart of the printer's craft, takes place at the zenith of the building. Later, Abbott describes at length the work of the compositor, in whom he witnesses a miraculous marriage of artisanal integrity and manufacturing efficiency:

He does not look at the face of the type to see what letter it is when he takes it up and sets it in the composing-stick, but takes it for granted, if it comes from the right compartment, it is the right letter. He has not time to look at it more than to give it a slight glance to see that he puts it into the composing-stick right end up. . . . [A] man, in order to set up a thousand ems [a unit of typographic measure, a typical letter space] in an hour, has to take up and place three thousand different pieces of metal. And when we consider that he has to select all these separate pieces from a great many different compartments, no less than one hundred and forty in all . . . it is plain his movements must be very active.

Printed by unfeeling machines, shipped from factories in bales and stacks, the book is no longer the work of an artisan. Its origins are mystified, bound up in electromechanical processes worthy of Frankenstein's workshop. The book now is a simple commodity—but like most modern commodities, it is opaque to its user, who has no idea how to make one himself. And yet, as Abbott reveals, for all the electroplating and the steam-impelled dexterity of the presses, it is the fingers of craftspeople that advance the book into the machine age.

AS THE MASS-PRODUCED BOOK FLOURISHED, the British Museum, like national libraries throughout Europe and in America, suddenly bloomed with books by the hundreds of thousands. The unlikely person who would preside over this boom at the Library of the British Museum—and become the nineteenth century's first librarian-Prometheus in the process—began his career as an exiled Italian revolutionary. A rising young lawyer, Antonio Panizzi antagonized the ducal government of his native Modena with his attachment to secret societies that mixed liberal politics with quasi-Masonic mysticism (this attraction to progressive ideology and esoteric knowledge perhaps prefigures Panizzi's career as a librarian). When show trials convicted comrades of treason, Panizzi escaped over the Alps and in 1823 published an account of the trials that earned him a death sentence in absentia and the guarantee of a life of exile. Panizzi eventually arrived in London; penniless, unable to speak the language, and repelled by the expatriates' bohemian demimonde, he made his way teaching Italian language and history. The teaching improved his English, while his revolutionary bona fides attracted powerful patrons; soon he was lecturing on the Renaissance, publishing scholarly articles in the *Edinburgh Review*, and joining the faculty of the newly established University of London. Although the professorial appointment cemented Panizzi's place in his adopted country, it did little to support him: a professor's salary was paid out of student fees, and at the practically minded University of London, few students had time for lectures on the Renaissance. Panizzi was happy to accept the recommendation of a well-placed friend to become an assistant librarian of the British Museum in 1831; his salary, "for five days in the week," amounted to two hundred pounds per year.

Panizzi quickly settled into the work that would assure his importance in the history of the British Library: cataloging. The library's first printed catalog, which appeared in 1810, ran to seven volumes. Like all catalogs of its day, it was simply an alphabetical list of the books in the library, which served the librarians as an inventory of the books in their charge. Each year, most libraries would close for a few weeks, to permit the librarians to run down the list and ensure that each book was still in its place on the shelf. Catalogs were designed for little else. Readers, after all, generally came to the library prepared; they knew what books they wanted to see, and what they wanted to find in them.

Yet between the time that first catalog was compiled and Panizzi's arrival at the British Museum, the number of books in its collections had increased by an order of magnitude. The original seven-volume catalog had been stuffed by librarians with scribbled additions and addenda; its interleavings had swollen it to forty-eight volumes. Plainly, a new catalog was needed. Panizzi, who had already made his reputation within the library by cataloging a collection of impossibly complicated tracts from the English Civil War, was the librarian best prepared to tackle the job.

What Panizzi's labors with obscure pamphlets had shown him

was the dense web of connections authors and publishers forged among works in print. Tracts answered other tracts, which might be reprintings of articles that had appeared in journals and newspapers, or excerpts from books; they could appear simultaneously in several forms, under several imprints. Such crucial information as the author's name, the publisher, and the date and place of publication might be incomplete, erroneous, or missing altogether. Panizzi developed a series of rules that reproduced these relations in the catalog, so that librarians—and crucially, readers—could trace and follow them. Unwittingly at first, he was helping to transform the library catalog from an inventory into an instrument of discovery. It's tempting to say that his discovery of intertextuality among even the most mundane books forebodes the rise of the interconnected world of the digital age; it's probably more accurate, however, to note that, from the vantage point of the wired world, Panizzi's catalog looks like the beginnings of the Internet.

Placed in charge of the effort to compile a new catalog, Panizzi employed these lessons from the start. No partial revision would suffice; he suggested a complete recataloging instead, in order to ensure internal consistency in the finished edition. He went abroad, too, to learn how other libraries made their catalogs. Although Panizzi still had a price on his head, he was now long removed from the early days of his exile, when the government of Modena would mail him advance bills for the cost of his own execution. From his tour of Continental Europe, he returned with a firm conception of the work at hand: "the first and chief object of a Catalogue," he announced in an 1836 report to the museum's trustees, is "easy access to the works which form part of the collection." This was not a tool for the librarians, moreover, but an instrument that "the public have the right to expect in such an institution." Though Panizzi would seem to have traveled far from his radical roots in Italy, his work was informed all along by a democratic impulse, as he makes clear in this report. "I want the poor student to have the same means of indulging his learned curiosity," he wrote the trustees, "of following his rational pursuits, of consulting the same authorities, of fathoming the most intricate inquiry as the richest man in the kingdom . . . and I contend that the government is bound to give him the most liberal and unlimited assistance in this respect." To Panizzi, the humble library catalog could be more than a list, more even than a guide to knowledge: it could be the means to transform society itself.

Panizzi was appointed Keeper of Printed Books in 1837; and seven years later, the first volume of the catalog, covering the letter *A*, had only just been published. Not everyone was pleased. "The exotic capriccios of a Librarian . . . should [not] be allowed to delay progress . . . [of] a practical Catalogue," wrote one Sir Nicholas Harris Nicolas, a learned gentleman with a fondness for naval history, who published in the *Spectator* a series of articles condemning the new catalog in 1846. Furthermore, he charged that Panizzi's catalog was "formed on so abstruse a plan as to require *ninety-one* rules for its construction; most, if not all, of which must be committed to memory, before any person can be aware under what head he will find even the commonest book in our language."

Nicolas was jealous of the influence of Panizzi in the library; his crude dig at the librarian's "exotic capriccios" betrays his suspicion of the Italian-born librarian (elsewhere he wonders whether Panizzi "intend[s] to insult the common sense of the country which has had the honour of adopting him"). But Nicolas is concerned about more than the catalog's delayed publication, its cumbrous weight, or its ultimate complexity: he is afraid that it will make the reader do more work.

Early in the project, Panizzi had chosen to add the "pressmark" of each book to its entry in the catalog. Like a call number on a modern library book, the gnomic pressmark indicated precisely the place where the book was to be found among the shelves of the library stacks (or "presses," as bookshelves were commonly called). Unlike call numbers, however, pressmarks referred not to a scheme of knowledge, but to a location; they are not classifications, but only coordinates. Panizzi explained the formulation of pressmarks, and their meaning, in his response to Nicolas: the pressmark "500 *a*," for instance, "means that the work itself is in the press which is numbered 500, and on the shelf of that press which is distinguished by the letter *a*; if the mark be 500 *a* 2, the meaning is that the work occupies the second place on that shelf; and if marked 500 *a*/6 2, that it is the sixth article in the 2nd vol. on shelf *a* of press 500." By providing such tutorials, Panizzi wanted to make the library transparent to readers—to replace the mysteries of its workings with a sophistication that would increase a reader's independence. In previous practice, a reader would simply request a book by title, and the librarians would find its pressmark in their own copy of the catalog in order to fetch it; the book would seem to appear magically as if sprung from the brow of Zeus. Now readers would be required to know the pressmark and to include it on the filled-out ticket they presented to librarians at the desk in order to request books. Nicolas realized that readers in quest of even the most common book, say, Hume's *History of England*, would have to make a trip to the catalog to look up its pressmark. "We know the inconvenience attending this obligation is felt by many literary men," he wrote, "whose time is of value to them. . . . [I]n a public library no more should be expected of a Reader than to specify the book he wants by its title, and that all besides belongs to the librarian." Nicolas sensed that Panizzi was trying to produce not only a new kind of catalog but a new kind of reader as well—one more independent, more knowledgeable of library systems—and he wished to play no part in the revolution.

Nicolas disliked the thought of thumbing more than forty-eight volumes of catalog to find his books. He scarcely could have imagined how fundamentally Panizzi's reforms would change the very idea of the catalog—not to mention its sheer bulk—in the years to come. If the devil had sent him along with Enoch Soames to visit the Round Reading Room of the British Library in 1991, he would have found that the copy of the printed catalog in use there, with its numerous supplements and additions, had swollen to a daunting twenty-three hundred volumes ringing the central desk.

Nicolas was not the only one who struggled with changes in the operation of the library. Complaints about delays in the delivery of books to readers increased, as did comments about the brusqueness of the staff; a reader named Charles Wilcox was sentenced to twelve months in jail for removing a book from the reading rooms. Letters to the *Times* registered dismay at the long waits, short hours, and delays in the appearance of the new catalog. But conflict was unavoidable: from 1830 to 1840, the number of registered readers grew from 3,000 to 16,000, according to P. R. Harris's *History of the British Museum Library*. Some 200,000 different books were ordered by those readers in a single year. Throughout the 1840s, however, the number of readers served each day remained steady, averaging about 230—close to the maximum the reading rooms could hold. Things were tight and tense in the Library of the British Museum as Panizzi's monumental catalog lurched toward completion.

All the fulminations of Nicolas and others hardly checked Panizzi's progress, however, or his zeal. In 1846, he published his reply to Harris in a book called *On the Supply of Printed Books from the Library to the Reading Room of the British Museum*. There he made clear the challenges the library faced in absorbing growing numbers of books and readers, and he pulled a sly joke on Nicolas, too, reprinting a letter he had sent early in Panizzi's tenure praising the librarian's initial reforms. Panizzi's antagonists fought back, and in 1847 a royal commission opened an investigation into patrons' complaints about the library and the museum. A highlight of the proceedings was the testimony of the formidable Thomas Carlyle, who joined Nicolas and others in condemning efforts to produce a new catalog. "Elaborate catalogues are not what we require," he scolded the commission, "but legible catalogues accessible to everybody." But when asked about his use of English Civil War tracts in the library, he commended their cataloging, saying that he had "succeeded in getting great benefit from them." This marked a victory for Panizzi, whose cataloging of those very tracts had served as the basis of the new methodology.

Ultimately, the royal commission vindicated Panizzi's policies and allowed him to proceed more or less unhindered. Panizzi's cataloging effort ceased to aim at a single publication and became instead an ongoing effort, as cataloging is in all libraries to this day.

Panizzi's reign at the museum lasted until 1866. He presided over the building of the monumental Round Reading Room (the design of which was based on his own pencil-sketch plan). In 1856 he became principal librarian; in 1869 he was knighted. His cataloging rules held sway in the British Museum well into the 1950s.

Sir Anthony Panizzi, the capricious, Promethean Italian revolutionary, had honored the common sense of the country of his adoption, and had created—not only for its learned lords but for its poor students, for its people, too—one of the greatest libraries in the world.

WHILE PANIZZI WAS ENGAGED in the Promethean project of building a library for the nation, many millions of its people were mired in poverty. It was in these years of class conflict and economic terror that the public library movement swept through Britain, as the nation's progressive elite recognized that the light of cultural and intellectual energy was lacking in the lives of commoners. The Napoleonic Wars had ground away at the British economy, and a host of stifling taxes and laws placed the greatest burdens on the working class. In 1838, the second of two years of depression, the London radical William Lovett offered Parliament a bill he called the People's Charter. Its six points, which included universal male suffrage and the end of property qualifications for election to government, were aimed at making Parliament answerable to a wider segment of Britain's growing population than ever before. Parliament rejected Lovett's bill, but the Chartist movement was born; it would articulate the hopes of Britain's working poor through the revolutionary year of 1848.

Like the dissenting churchmen two hundred years before, the Chartists recognized the importance of education in fulfilling the aspirations of those excluded from power and position. Throughout Britain in the mid-nineteenth century, Chartist reading rooms—cooperative lending libraries offering books to members of radical organizations—sprang up. These proved extremely popular and soon competed with commercially minded subscription libraries, which for a typically modest fee offered their members access to an ever-changing list of books. The threat to established order did not go unnoticed; *Blackwood's Magazine* in 1825 had proclaimed that "whenever the lower order of any state have obtained a smattering of knowledge they have generally used it to produce national ruin." The trade unionist Francis Place, however, argued that reading would bring the radical poor into the circle of culture, decency, and prosperity, and turn them away from the enticements of the mob. "As a man's understanding is directed to some laudable pursuit, his desire for information will increase; he will become decent in his conduct and language, sober, discreet.... [S]uch a man will frequently rise as the uninformed man sinks."

Although utilitarian philosophers like Jeremy Bentham and his disciple John Stuart Mill were repelled by radical tactics, they supported Place's view that greater access to information would benefit society as a whole. Mill said that the masses were "bad calculators" who "lacked practical good sense," and that a sound education would turn them into good calculators: sober and sensible consumers, well-trained and aspiring workers. Among a class of intellectuals who had begun to believe that economic phenomena followed the universal laws revealed by reason, it made sense that by greater access to information, all people could be trained in reason's principles, turning themselves into rational actors for the greater good of all. As the library historian Alistair Black puts it, "through assimilation of the powers of reason, fostered by education, the masses would come to accept capitalist principles as truth. Education ... taught men and women to buy in the cheapest markets and sell in the most expensive, ... in effect, how to be 'at one' with the acquisitive nature of capitalist society." Turning out such "good calculators" was the aim of utilitarian education, and the tradesmen's reading rooms and subscription libraries offered the possibility of doing so in an economical fashion. For in a well-tended library, the utilitarians realized, each book's value to society increases as more people gain access to and use it. Unlike the private book, whose functional use ends when it is read and placed on the shelf for the last time, a library book may continue to open doors.

But not all the utilitarians were coldly economical in their calculations. John Stuart Mill in particular, inspired by the Romantic movement, felt that libraries offered a greater good than reason: they offered happiness as well. Books offered more than opportunities for training, for indoctrination into the culture of capitalism. They offered an escape, however momentary; they offered repose and reflection, which ultimately encouraged the regard for one's fellow man that is the foundation of altruism.

All this from libraries! So the sponsors of the 1850 public library bill perhaps hoped when they persuaded Parliament to pass it. Alistair Black charts the influence of utilitarian thinking on supporters of public libraries, suggesting that their motives might have been, well, more utilitarian: they hoped that libraries would channel the subversive urges of an underclass traditionally denied access to cultural means. In any case, the tax-supported public libraries quickly supplanted the subscription libraries and Chartist reading rooms. When the Manchester Public Library opened in 1852, it occupied a former Chartist hall, and speakers at the opening ceremony couched their comments in the language of class war and reconciliation. The library promoter Joseph Brotherton hoped that all classes "would learn how necessary they were to each other—how labour and capital were bound together by a link, and how the interests of all classes, rich and poor, were intertwined, like the ivy and the oak." No less a light than Charles Dickens, who spoke as well, was confident that libraries would teach "that capital and labour are not opposed, but mutually dependant and mutually supporting."

EUROPE'S REVOLUTIONARY PANGS were felt in America, too, if in diluted form. The parents of Melville Louis Kossuth Dewey, in fact, named their son after after the Hungarian reformer Lajos Kossuth, who in exile after his country's 1848 revolution proved immensely popular as a lecturer. Social upheavals across Europe in that year seemed to promise an end to monarchies, and for a time they captured the imagination of Americans predisposed to judge hereditary rulers harshly. Revolutionaries were especially valued, however, in the northwestern corner of upstate New York where Dewey was born in 1851; it is still called the Burned-over District, for the number of religious revolutions, starting with Mormonism, that have kindled their first flames in the area. As a proponent of simplified spelling, Dewey eventually dropped his foreign-inspired middle name and shortened the spelling of his given name to Melvil. But as a librarian, educator, and social reformer, he would embody the fervor and moral certitude of the Burned-over District in all its contradictory impulses.

Young Melville's own ambitions were sparked by a real fire. When his school caught fire in 1868, Dewey found himself rescuing books from the smoldering library, inhaling a great deal of smoke in the process. The deep cough he developed afterward led his doctor to conclude that he would be dead within two years. According to his biographer Wayne Wiegand, this early awareness of imminent death spurred an interest in time-saving that lasted the rest of Dewey's life, and provided the pattern for all his reforms. In everything from the training of library staff to the shelving of books, efficiency was Dewey's lodestone. Efficiency became his obsession; he championed phonetic spelling, shorthand, and the metric system, believing that the key to unlocking enormous resources of time resided in a rationalizing simplicity.

Dewey's greatest contribution—the one for which he is best known—came while he was still a student at Amherst College. Working as a library assistant, Dewey found himself frustrated by the collection's disorganization. He set about devising a system by which he might bring order to the books. The concern for classification itself did not originate with Dewey; indeed, it was a main topic among librarians of the day. Libraries were growing rapidly. The old system, in which each book was assigned a fixed spot on a shelf, would no longer do; each new addition of books required an overhaul of the entire catalog. In St. Louis, William Torrey Harris had hit upon the idea of classifying not the books but the knowledge they contained; such a system provided a scheme of relative classification, in which books were found according to their relationship to one another. Harris followed Bacon's tripartite theory of knowledge, sorting books according to the disciplines of history, poetry, and philosophy. These branches of learning were amenable to further analysis, allowing an elaboration of the structure of knowledge that would cover all works of the mind. Although intellectuals had known and used such classificatory schemes since the Middle Ages, they had applied them to libraries only rarely, and typically in sketchy and general terms (the Vatican Library, with its tables divided according to the sacred and the profane, provides an example of one such rough scheme). In nineteenth-century libraries, meanwhile, systems had been developed like that used by the British Museum, in which the shelves were given numerical "names" that could be more or less arbitrarily divided up to note the location of specific books. Dewey's innovation was to marry the two systems, the epistemological and the numerical. The numbers didn't just designate a shelving system; they differentiated among fields of knowledge. Thus he joined the analytical simplicity of decimal numbers to an intuitive scheme of knowledge, one that would fluidly accommodate all the books ever written, and all the books that could be written as well.

But the "decimal classification," for all its manifold impact on libraries and our experience of them, hardly exhausts Dewey's influence on the library world. Indeed, nearly every aspect of it bears his stamp: he pioneered the systematic education of librarians, founding the first library school at Columbia in 1889; he launched a company, the Library Bureau, to peddle furniture and office supplies (and an entire, efficiency-minded aesthetic of interior design) to libraries big and small; in helping to found the American Library Association, he set standards for the profession, both internal (that is to say, in terms of expected education, ethics, and standards of work) and external (the role of the librarian in society as a whole). Dewey's vigor, zeal, and indomitable personality contributed as much as the classification that bears his name to making him the most famous librarian of his or any other time. In many respects, this is unfortunate, for Dewey's obsession with efficiency, his reliance on the mandate of authority and hierarchy, and his sociocultural and religious prejudices affected the development of the library in ways that haunt it to this day.

In a sense, Dewey could be called the John Adams of the American library movement. He combined Adams's pugnacious determination and strength in political battle with a sense of right and duty to authority. When the first meeting of the American Library Association (ALA) convened in 1876, Dewey was present; at twenty-five, he was the youngest member of a group that included the Boston Public Library director Justin Winsor (later Librarian of Harvard College) and William Frederick Poole, author of *Poole's Index to Periodical Literature*, the first such resource. From the start, Dewey strove to define the profession and the work of the association in his own efficiency-minded terms—often in sharp distinction to the vision put forth by scholar-librarians like Winsor and Poole. He shared their vision of the importance of reading to social progress, but his views of how gains were to be made could hardly have been more different from theirs.

At the conference, the scholar-librarians discussed what kinds of readers the library might properly host, and what kinds of books those readers should be permitted to use. Such emphasis was new for librarians. Previously, the extent and nature of collections was pretty well understood: it was part of the cultural patrimony handed down from antiquity. But now new kinds of books were being produced, as publishers took advantage of cheap paper and mass production methods to reach out and create new readers for their wares. The reform-minded librarians wished to interpose themselves between the masses and the books, to provide guidance in appropriate kinds of reading. Dewey agreed with this motive. But he felt that to achieve it, libraries needed to focus less on the titles of the books they chose and more on the ways in which they organized those books and made them available. To a very great extent, this was a matter of the standardization of everything: not only the cataloging schemes but the size of cards and cabinets used in catalogs should be the same in all libraries. As Dewey wrote in the first issue of the *American Library Journal*, "[c]ataloguing, indexing, and the score of things which admit it, are to be done *once* for all the libraries, at a vast reduction to each institution. . . . [A] much larger percentage of the income is therefore made available for the books." In essence, though, Dewey was thinking about libraries everywhere, and indeed he hoped libraries would be established in even the smallest communities to serve the most marginal populations. He really had a single, ideal library in mind. As his biographer Wiegand phrases it, "he was convinced the best way to maximize the library's potential was to create effectively uniform collections of quality materials and increase service efficiency by standardizing internal library procedures with common forms, appliances, and rules and systems of arrangement." A visitor to a library organized along Dewey's lines finds her way around without difficulty. To Dewey, local interests and special needs were less important than the efficient movement of books into the hands of readers. And while his undying and eccentric reliance on the bromide of efficiency undeniably led libraries to greater economies—adopting not only his furniture and his system of classification but the newly invented card catalog as well—such reform came at the cost of the sort of local diversity that makes individual libraries worth visiting, and reading in.

This last innovation, the card catalog, was not Dewey's invention. Perhaps the first prominent card catalog was Edward Gibbon's inventory on playing cards. By the middle of the nineteenth century, cards were already in common use by librarians who faced unmanageably messy, addenda-addled inventories. In the early part of the century, an eccentric named William Coswell was retained by Harvard College to compile a new catalog. He hit upon the idea of cutting the old catalogs into strips and sorting the individual entries into groups by subject. This work became the basis of a "slip catalog" that made the librarian's yearly review of the collection much easier. Harvard did not use cards to make a public catalog—the first card catalog, in fact, as we think of it today—until 1860. The use of cards quickly caught on, however, and became standardized; the pages of Dewey's Library Bureau *Catalog* are stuffed with cards, cases, specialized typewriters, and other tools for the maintenance of card catalogs.

But Dewey sought to standardize not only catalogs but all aspects of the library experience. Again, it's among the pages of the Library Bureau's *Catalog* that Dewey's controlling vision reveals itself: here are the tables, the map stands, the shelves, the charge desks and date stamps, the inkwells and the pens, which the turn-of-the-century librarian could depend upon to furnish the most efficient library possible. Chairs exhibit simple, elegant lines, with narrow, unadorned legs and open structure to prevent the collection of dust beneath the seat. Patented bookshelves, braces, and labels made the browsing of books uniform from library to library. Under Dewey's inspiration, the tools of library economy proliferated into a host of specialized labels, pockets, stationery, pen nibs, and sundry other supplies. The catalog provided the means to turn any drowsy village library into an efficient engine for putting books into people's hands, an early machine age reader's utopia.

49

26h. Pencil Dater. A movable pad dater attached to a lead pencil; a slight motion of the hand stamps the date much plainer than it can be written, without removing the hand from the pencil. Of great service at the loan desk, where books must be charged rapidly. Devised at the Milwaukee Public Library, and adopted by many others.

Price, dater and L. B. dates, complete, 75c.

26i2. L. B. Accession and Numbering Stamp. Used in library work for registering the accession number in books, on cards, and elsewhere, and in banks and commercial offices for numbering checks, stock certificates, etc. This machine is very exact in its operation. The figures shift automatically one number higher at each impression, as required for consecutive numbering or paging, or it can be instantly adjusted to print each number twice, or to repeat the same number indefinitely. Made specially for us. We recommend them as the best obtainable.

Selection can be made from the following face type:—

d) №1234567890

e) №1234567890

f) №1234567890

g) №1234567890

h) №1234567890

PRICES.

4-wheel Machine, numbering from 1 to 9999,	.	.	**$25.00**
5-wheel	" " 99999,	.	**30.00**
6-wheel	" " 999999,	.	**35.00**

26i3. D. C. Numbering Stamp. For users of the Decimal Classification a special stamp has been made, providing for two decimals; i. e. for five figures of the classification. Used for printing the class numbers on cards, book plates, and labels. It has not only proved a genuine labor-saver, but adds uniformity and legibility to the catalog.

Price, 26i3 5-wheel, D. C. Stamp **$30.00**

A slight motion of the hand. Labor-saving devices depicted in the Library Bureau's 1890 Catalog. Widener Library B 7770.8.5.

One of the Library Bureau *Catalog*'s most striking details, however, is its organization. Like the books in Dewey's libraries, the products in his mercantile catalogs also conformed to the decimal system. A table at the front listed not the pages on which newspaper wands, catalog card typewriters, and atlas stands could be found, but their respective classifications. The 20s, for example, were devoted to "Technical Fittings." Within the 20s, stamps and daters were accorded the 26s; from there, the system turns alphabetical. As in the library, the class system in the catalog frustrated the reader, but with a purpose: to reward and encourage browsing instead. Other library reformers talked about the similarity between the library reader and the shopper; for Dewey, this was no metaphor.

Dewey's attitude toward women provides another example of his mixed impact on the library world. The Boston Athenaeum had been the first library to employ women in 1857; this was yet another innovation Dewey seized upon and made his own. The school he founded at Columbia, the School of Library Economy, admitted women to its first class. Dewey took this step without consulting the university trustees, and it was the single most important factor in their decision to close the school just two years later (Dewey moved the school to the state university at Albany). In superficial retrospect, the decision looks like a pioneer move in women's rights. But as his biographer Wiegand points out, Dewey actually used the admittance of women to the college to the same end he used their hiring in the library: to define the profession down. Women were already socially subordinate to the men who filled faculty roles; for Dewey, this subordination nicely mirrored the professional subordination of librarians to professors and other experts—a subordination he deemed necessary to the efficient workings of the library. While his colleagues in the ALA cultivated the authority to direct the reading of their patrons, Dewey eschewed this mandate. Library workers, after all, were far too busy cataloging books and putting them in patrons' hands to trouble themselves with the choosing of books. As Wiegand puts it, Dewey didn't realize that he effectively "robbed librarianship of a direct claim to the 'authority' to determine 'best reading,' thus significantly limiting its power in the world of professions."

For other librarians of Dewey's time, by contrast, optimism about their calling—their authority to determine "best reading"— was paramount. Even outside the circle of the profession, the Promethean impulse to improve the cultural lot of all mankind had already manifested itself as an ethical imperative to manage the flow of books into readers' hands. No less a figure than Ralph Waldo Emerson concerned himself with the challenges students, like all new readers, faced in the nineteenth century's burgeoning library. Writing in a report to Harvard's trustees in 1868, Emerson noted that a new figure, a "Professor of Books," was needed to serve as guide within the labyrinth of groaning shelves. Students flee the library, he wrote,

> repelled by the multitude of books which speak to them of their own ignorance,—their very multitude concealing from the gazing youth . . . the very information & learning he wants. Would some kind scholar take pity on his sincere curiosity, & . . . guide him to the class of works & presently to the precise author who has written as for him alone. Could not a gentleman be found to occupy a desk . . . as the *Library Counsellor*, to whom the Librarian could refer inquiries on authors & subjects?

Emerson's pity for the plight of the Harvard College student mirrors the concern of nineteenth-century librarians for all lost readers. And just as mythology tells us how Prometheus's pity was born of his love for mankind, so do the myths contained in the very first volume of the *American Library Journal* offer oracular visions of librarians laboring to shape the experiences and, ultimately, the minds of readers.

Americans through the Colonial and Federal periods were highly literate. In 1731, Benjamin Franklin and members of his "Junto," a Philadelphia literary soceity, formed the Library Company, offering access to books for the community; the Boston Athenaeum was founded in 1807. Throughout this time, libraries and literary circles sprang up in cities large and small, some wildly democratic, others self-consciously elitist. But American soceity grew and changed in the early 1800s; by midcentury, the descendants of those early literati were as concerned as their European counterparts with a perceived decline in the reading standards of the public at large.

Charles Francis Adams, for instance, who administered the public library in Quincy, Massachusetts, strikes a familiar note when he reminds his colleagues that the common schools have taught the public "to read, but [not] *how* to read." The dangers to libraries presented by this unmoored proficiency were clear. In an article in the inaugural issue of the *American Library Journal,* Adams describes how the opportunities the free library offers will overwhelm the masses; dismayed by the variety of reading material, unprepared to find and read the best and most beautiful books, they will depart unfulfilled and take their potential with them. In depicting the danger and the difficulty, Adams adopts the metaphor of addiction. "It is so very easy," he says, "and so very pleasant too, to read only books which lead to nothing, light and interesting books, and the more the better, that it is almost as difficult to wean ourselves from it as from the habit of chewing tobacco to excess, or of smoking the whole time, or of depending for stimulus upon tea or coffee or spirits."

In the same issue, William Frederick Poole (who ran the Chicago Public Library) also draws a parallel between the smoking

and reading habits. To Poole, however, the tobacco reference was not
entirely negative. "I smoked tobacco and read Milton at the same
time," he declares, "and for the same motive: to find out what was the
recondite charm in them that gave my father so much pleasure." But
too many people, Poole admits, are dissuaded by that first unpleasant
impression of tobacco from any further consideration of its charms.
So it is with reading—too early a diet of overly strong stuff, and the
new reader will soon be an ex-reader. However Poole and Adams
may have differed over tobacco, they are in complete agreement
about the nature and development of habits of reading—against an
intellectual elite who hold the new library in contempt. It doesn't
have enough good books, the elite might say; it doesn't have enough
of *our* books. Indeed, there aren't enough such books, and the elite
will never write them fast enough, to survive dilution in the sea of
the cheap, the tawdry, the "highly seasoned." But Poole reminds elite
readers that their own tastes were not always so recondite.

> The scholar, in his pride of intellect, forgets the progressive steps
> he took in his own mental development—the stories read to him
> in the nursery, the boy's book of adventure in which he revelled
> with delight, and the sentimental novel over which he shed tears
> in his youth. [He] supposes that the masses will read books of his
> standard if they were not supplied with the books to which he
> objects; but he is mistaken. Shut up to this choice, they will read
> no books.

Later he writes,

> I have never met a person of much literary culture who would not
> confess that at some period in his life, usually in his youth, he had
> read novels excessively. . . . My observation . . . has confirmed me

in the belief that there is in the mental development of every person who later attains to literary culture a limited period when he craves novel-reading; and perhaps reads novels to excess; but from which, if the desire be gratified, he passes safely out into broader fields of study, and this craving never returns to him in its original form.

Here, the ontogeny of elite readers—the growth and development of their literary habit—suggests to Poole a whole ontology of reading in its ideal form. The vast generic range of reading in the nineteenth century, which publishers and entrepreneurial authors had turned into a kind of literary great chain of being reflecting the levels and stations of society and gender, is transformed here into a developmental process undergone by the individual reader under the management of the librarian. As the scholar began with nursery tales and progressed through adventure stories, romances, biography, travel, and history, so will the new readers develop, and their society along with them. And the correct parsing of each reader's place in this developmental scale is the special work of the librarian, the role he plays in patrons' lives. Nurses raise infants; librarians raise library patrons. Readers read books; librarians read readers.

In "The Qualifications of a Librarian," Lloyd P. Smith, of the Philadelphia Library Company, outlines drives and talents that fit the Promethean prototype. The librarian he describes is an intellectual demiurge, uniquely prepared to process the clay of untutored readers into the precious metals of a cultured elite. Learned in classical and modern languages, abreast of the latest scholarship across specialties, wise in the ways of attracting donors, firm in discipline and generous in amiability, Smith's librarian above all is a "*helluo librorum, a devourer of literature.*" No "teacher[s] wanting discipline" need apply. And these qualities are largely a matter of inheritance, as Smith tells us in another fit of Latinity: "*Custos librorum nascitur, non fit.* The love of literature . . . must be in the breed; a man must belong to the Brahmin caste." And what is the Brahmin in the late nineteenth century but a Titan in the mythological mold—a power of old, who stands between the people, on the one hand, and the captains of industry and administrators of a government ever more comprehensive, ramified, and intrusive, on the other. Smith's librarian may be a failed vicar or untenured professor, but for all his failings he is a man of science and learning, and culture is his birthright. This is the Prometheus who will bring the light of learning to the masses. To Smith, all the talents of this class must be brought to bear on the problems of setting a whole culture of readers right. All his tools are put to use in the pursuit of a single ideal, to make all reading serve an overarching purpose: the coordinated progress of society and the individual within it.

Perhaps the most magnificent imagining of the librarian's power to mold the readers in his charge comes in the form of a kind of dramatic manifesto by Samuel S. Green of the Worcester Free Public Library, in his essay "Personal Relations between Librarians and Readers." Green's narrative is episodic, minimalist: no more than a series of vignettes taken from a typical day in the librarian's life. In the character of his librarian, Green distills all the progressive zeal of Winsor, the good-hearted brio of Poole, and the patrician gravitas of Smith.

First, know your customer. "When scholars and persons of high social position [the old patrons of the library, in both senses of the word] come to a library, they have confidence enough. . . . Modest men in the humbler walks of life, and well-trained boys and girls, need encouragement before they become ready to say freely what they want." In the later episodes in the life of Green's librarian, however, it becomes clear that the problem isn't one of timidity but one of wisdom. It isn't that they can't utter what they want; in truth, they don't know what they need. And it's up to the librarian to remedy the deficiency. When craftsmen come to the library, they'll be looking for patterns and pictures; know the standard sources, and offer them up without undue comment. When a schoolgirl drops in looking for information about the origin of the yard measure, however, more pedagogical pressure should be applied, though lightly; only point the way to the likeliest sources, wait for the young reader to go astray, and then set her right. By such gentle guidance and experimentation, she will learn, in time, to find the way on her own. And yet for a citizen building a house, who is "crowded by business, but still glad to spend a single hour in the library," the approach is different: "the librarian must get the books which contain the desired information, and hand them to the reader open to the proper pages." The librarian is sensitive to the needs and capacities of his clients. Even in political disputes, Green makes clear how the librarian's offer of the right work to the right disputant might clear the way to resolution. Custodian of a new kind of library, he should keep his hand invisible even as it guides the progress of the community as a whole, his finger on the pulse of political and economic as well as cultural and literary needs and tastes. And sometimes, the librarian's own vast store of knowledge will suffice, without recourse to the collections of the library. " 'Is it true,' inquires a young lady, 'that the little bust we see so often, and which is generally called "Clyte," should be called "Clytie"? ' The librarian answers 'Yes.' " Surely, the librarian needed to consult no dictionaries to remember that Clytie was the nymph who, secretly loving Apollo, gazed so intently at the sun's passage through the sky that she turned into the heliotrope.

Like Henry Higgins in *My Fair Lady*, the librarian knows with the first word from a reader's mouth precisely the hamlet, neighborhood, or street he or she hails from in the geography of the intel-

BOOKS FOR ALL ✦ 151

lect. All roads from those diverse compass points lead, however, to the same eternal city, that of learning, progress, and refined sensibil-ity. By gaining the "respect and confidence" of this disparate mass of readers, the librarian is granted "opportunities of stimulating the love of study"; "you find out what books the actual users of the library need," and make the library more popular in the community thereby. The books of the library "have been provided for the use of persons of differing degrees of refinement and moral susceptibility, and for those who occupy mental planes of various attitudes." To Smith's catalog of qualifications, we must then add a razor-sharp social intelligence and awareness of the vagaries of human development.

Once again, this whole arsenal is brought to bear on a single problem: people don't read the right sort of books. The library is devoted to solving this ill, by any means necessary. "Place in the cir-culating department one of the most accomplished persons in the corps of your assistants," Green writes,

> some cultivated woman, for instance, who heartily enjoys works of the imagination, but whose taste is educated. . . . It is well if there is a vein of philanthropy in her composition. . . . Let the assistant, then, have some regular work, but such employment as she can at once lay aside when her aid is asked for in picking out books to read. . . . [L]et her aim at providing every person who applies for aid with the best book he is willing to read.

"The best book he is willing to read"—and if it takes a pretty assis-tant to induce him to read it, it's just as well. No inducement is out of bounds; persistence is the key. "A librarian should be as unwilling to allow an inquirer to leave the library with his question unan-swered as a shop-keeper is to have a customer go out of his store without making a purchase."

Like Smith, Green imagines a librarian in the patrician mold. But it's a patrician poised on the brink of a rupture between old and new, between the *custos librorum* of old and the information social worker of modernity. Contemporary librarians similarly are caught between the cultural inspirations of the old and the professional aspirations of the new. "Librarianship," begins the anonymous author of "Continuity," which appeared in an 1890 issue of *Harper's Weekly*, "offers a better field for mental gymnastics than any other profession." As we quickly discover, though, our hero is not a bit happy about it. He has neither the time nor the inclination to midwife a reader's inchoate urges into rarefied cultural tastes. This librarian is too busy for such heady intimacies; for while he sits at the front desk serving his patrons' every whim, he's also "cataloguing the four thousand and tenth of an interminable series of French plays." Despite this initial chagrin, the librarian seems to prefer this task to the answering of patrons' questions. When a "drove of unbroken sophomores comes prancing into the library," his wits are "jogged out of Paris and across a half-century," back from the milieu of Molière and into progressive library land. It's immediately clear that this librarian has no interest in the journey. Enter the sophomores:

> "Say, will you please give me a chart of Long Island Sound?"
> "Say, may I have all my books renewed?"
> "Say, can you tell me where Milton speaks of the Golden
> Chersonese?"
> "Say, will you show me something on the woodchuck?"
> "Say, is Professor Scribner in?"

This drove of sophomores seems tolerably well broken: they are, after all, unfailingly, if chorally, polite. But as the narrator struggles to master his disdain, he makes clear how deep is the divide between the two realms of his work: on the one hand, he revels in bibliographical, scholarly detective work; on the other, he is forced to play the part of the public servant, the functionary, the scrivener chained to the reference desk.

The sophomores depart, and the librarian returns to his bibliographical reveries: "here," he writes, "is a thin little pamphlet called *Les suites d'un marriage de raison. . . . par MM. Dartois, Leon Brunswick et Lhéric* [*sic*]. To catalogue it I must first of all identify authors. . . ." Soon, however, more patrons interrupt—and in "Continuity" the patrons are idiots, sharps, and malcontents. One man is trying to help his landlady raise gamecocks. Another needs help deciphering his own handwriting. A student thinks that Francis Bacon's *New Atlantis* is a magazine article, while another wants the librarian to write his thesis on Byron for him. Someone asks whether the librarian has any special "litterury" taste; another wants him to figure his board bill for him.

Despite the continual snapping of these vultures at his liver, the librarian slogs on. Eventually, he convinces himself that his playwright, Lhéris, is in fact one Lévy, pinpointing the crucial evidence as the waning sunlight that "breaks sorrowfully . . . through painted panes" mingles with the library's swirling dust. With this, the narrator gives his workplace the aura of a church—one in which the confessions beat the clergy about the head all day long and where no relief is to be found from the chanting of the psalms. "The little French play is finally catalogued," he writes in conclusion.

Author card, subject card, cross references, and all. Dartois and the brothers Lévy prove to have been quite fecund, and erelong their names as joint authors are intricately woven into the main catalogue. Then one day I discover by chance that Dartois really wrote his name François Victor Armand d'Artois de Bournonville, and I have all that work to go over again.

The librarian of this *Harper's* piece is the mirror image of the ideal presented by pioneers like Poole and Winsor. Presented—or beset—with the same set of problems, he refuses to convert the gamey scoffers' challenges into professional opportunities. Instead, he embraces all the vices the pioneers complained of in librarians of old: jealousy, disdain, resentment at his own low station in the transformed library—where the books are free to all, even the amnesiac, the impolitic, and the downright illiterate. Painfully aware of the changed context of library service, he refuses to fit into the progressive mold the profession offers.

As the Library Bureau *Catalog* for 1890 points out, the chief aim of the library's catalog is to help patrons find the books they want as quickly as possible. That's just what Panizzi, the first Promethean librarian, asserted when he began reforming the catalog of the British Museum at the beginning of the nineteenth century. But for this librarian at the end of the century, cataloging remains an end in itself, and the readers' searches for the right books only and always get in the way.

An earlier generation of his colleagues and mentors had developed the professional mythology by reimagining class-based differences in reading taste (which were already imaginary—for rich and poor alike enjoy the cheap, the tawdry, and the "highly seasoned") as stages in a developmental scheme. In the process, they reimagined themselves as intellectual physicians who would taxonomize the developmental processes of readers, and diagnose and treat their aberrations. In "Continuity," however, all that progressive mythology is jettisoned. What remains is a social atomism in which each reader is cut off from others, and the librarian cut off from them all. The characters of "Continuity" are mired in their own foibles, and the librarian is distinctly modern in his awareness of this as he toils to create catalogs for readers who lack the intellectual wherewithal to make use of them. Librarians couldn't hope to guide the people in their use of such titanic gifts as literacy and access to information. Ultimately, they could hardly lend a hand in the shaping of cultural tastes, for these move at the whim of larger and more climatic forces: all the manifold urges, distractions, and obstructions of modern life.

CHAPTER SIX

Knowledge on Fire

If the nineteenth century was about the building of libraries, the twentieth was about their destruction. Book burning wasn't invented in the twentieth century, of course; it stalks the history of the library from Alexandria to Tenochtitlán, from Cappadocia to Catalonia, from China's Qin dynasty to the dissolution of the English monasteries. Nonetheless, it was in the twentieth century that new ways of destroying books, and of exploiting their destruction, were tested and refined. It may not be too much to say that the sudden disembodiment of the book in the late twentieth century—as text disappeared first into the grainy obfuscations of microfilm and eventually into the pixelated ether of the Internet—began with crude renewals of violence against the book in the First and Second World Wars. Heinrich Heine's observation "There where one burns books one in the end burns men" is often invoked in accounts of latter-day biblioclasm, especially of the Nazi book burnings of May

1933. Yet Heine was a person of the nineteenth century, writing (in *Almansor, eine Tragödie*) about the burning of books in fifteenth-century Spain and Portugal. But in the last century, one of total ideology and total war, it became clear that burning a library is not the only way to destroy it.

ON AUGUST 25, 1914, less than two weeks into their drive across Belgium, German troops entered the university town of Louvain. The Belgian army made no attempt to defend what had been declared an "open city" in recognition of its unique trove of Gothic art and architecture and its university's glorious library. Once ruled by the dukes of Brabant, medieval Louvain had been home to a thriving textile industry, which by the fifteenth century had begun to decline. The town was rescued from economic oblivion by a 1425 papal bull granting a university charter. The new University of Louvain drew its students not only from the Low Countries but from France and Germany as well, and the town quickly became a cosmopolitan center of lettered culture. In part because of the university's need for books, Louvain also became the seat of printing in Belgium; the first Belgian printer, Jean de Westphalie, produced some half a dozen books a year there from 1474 until 1496. Since printers came under the juridical protection of the rector of the university, the town became a safe haven for the book trade, relatively free from official censorship and the fickle pressures of royal patrons. This Flemish town of spires and bookshops attracted important scholars, most notably Erasmus, who called Louvain home from 1517 to 1521. Although never formally attached to the university, he helped found a humanist College of Three Languages there, which featured rigorous philological instruction in Hebrew, Greek, and Latin. The university's small library began to grow during this time, mostly with the products of the Louvain book trade. But the books would wait for a building of their own until 1730, when a gift of 3,500 volumes suddenly swelled the faculty collection. By August 1914, the library contained some 70,000 volumes and 300 manuscripts, the fruit of almost five hundred years of uninterrupted intellectual life. Among the holdings of the library were 350 incunabula, a series of editions of early printed Bibles, a mass of rare Jesuitica, a copious body of materials relating to religious reform in the Low Countries, political pamphlets from the Thirty Years' War and the invasion of Belgium by Louis XIV, archives, autograph manuscripts of Thomas à Kempis, and the university's own significant archives.

As the German invasion reached Louvain, outraged civilians began to strike back at the occupying troops. The German response was swift and awful. "There had been a series of savage reprisals on villages east of Louvain," the *New York Times* reported on August 30, "and part of Tieremont had been burned by the German troops." To forestall civilan attacks, the German army upon entering Louvain took "three hostages, the Burgomaster and two eminent citizens . . . the son of one of the hostages, a boy of 15 or 16 years old, stood talking to the German commandant. . . . Suddenly the boy drew a revolver and shot the German dead." This shot was evidently a signal to partisans watching nearby: "immediately concerted firing is said to have begun from the roofs and windows surrounding the square." But Belgian witnesses told a different story: German troops, retreating "in disorder," mistakenly fired on their comrades in Louvain, resulting in several German deaths (reported in the *Times*, with a London dateline of August 28).

Whoever fired on their soldiers, the Germans decided to make an example of Louvain. First they shot their hostages. Next "the inhabitants were ordered out of their homes . . . and soldiers furnished with bombs set fire to all parts of the city." Louvain's peerless Gothic architecture, its unique art treasures, and its remarkable library were utterly destroyed. "The city," reported the *Times*, "which had a population of 45,000, and was the intellectual metropolis of the Low Countries, is now nothing more than a heap of ashes."

Alleging that Belgian civilians had committed such atrocities as ambushing rearguard troops and gouging out the eyes of wounded soldiers in the field, the German government justified the burning of Louvain on grounds of military necessity. "The barbarous attitude of the Belgian population in all parts occupied by our troops has not only justified our severest measures," the Germans declared, "but forced them on us for the sake of self-preservation." The West, of course, saw it differently. "It is treason to civilization," wrote the London *Daily Chronicle* on August 29. "War on non-combatants is bad enough, but this is war on posterity to the remotest generations." Eight days after the Germans razed the town, a witness wrote that "even into the country, leaves of manuscripts and books fluttered about, half burned, at the mercy of the wind." One manuscript was saved, though: a professor had withdrawn it for consultation and carried it with him when he fled the city before the German occupation. Trudging along in a refugee column, he stopped in a garden near Ghent and buried the book, "enclosed in a little iron safe." There is no record of this single manuscript's return to the library or of its rediscovery. Perhaps the last book of Louvain's great prewar library still rests in its iron casket, a hidden library of one.

Not long after the war ended, a group of American donors established a committee to rebuild the library, raising funds and engaging the architect Whitney Warren to design a new building. But the project ran into controversy from the start. Cardinal Mercier, the archbishop of Malines, who presided over Louvain and its university, had provided Warren the text for an inscription to be placed on the balustrade: *Furore Teutonico Diruta / Dono Americano Restituta* (destroyed by German fury, rebuilt by American generosity). The cardinal died before the library was built, however, and the university rector, Monseigneur Ladeuze, considered the inscription inappropriate. German students, after all, had always figured among the student body, and the faculty depended on collegial contacts with German peers. Ladeuze felt that jingoism was not part of the mission of a university; it should serve instead as a repository and nursery for the lettered culture Europeans of all nations held in common.

But Cardinal Mercier's sentimental impulse had already infected Warren's design for the library. A pamphlet published by the American committee announced that the imagery on the façade would focus "on the figure of Our Lady of Victory, supported by St. George and St. Michael crushing the Evil Spirits." The plans for decoration also included a scene of the destruction of the library and busts of war heroes, "the King, the Queen, and Cardinal Mercier." The balustrade with its inscription describing German infamy would include "the coats of arms of Belgium and the United States." Above all this, a carillon was to rise, for chimes were "universal in all Flemish towns." This one, however, was to be unique: "Hourly, . . . [it] will ring forth the national airs of those nations who fought in the Great War, that Honour, Right, and Justice might survive—'The Star Spangled Banner,' the 'Marseillaise,' 'God Save the King,' the 'Brabançonne,' etc."

Horrified by the thought of turning his library into a jingoist's music box, however, Rector Ladeuze lobbied fiercely for restraint. The library that was eventually built followed Warren's basic plan, but lacked all the jingoistic elements the late Cardinal Mercier might have liked: the national anthem–playing carillon, the victors' coats of arms, the inscription decrying German fury. The pamphlet had stated that the bell tower of the new library would "dominate the surrounding country"—in this detail, and nearly this alone, were the American committee's fond hopes fulfilled.

Ladeuze died on the eve of World War II, rector of a university and a library that reflected his own humanist outlook. When German troops once again rolled through Belgium on May 16, 1940, their first sight of Louvain was that library tower rising over the trees and rooftops of the city. Already, another generation of Louvainers had fled under relentless German bombardment; this time, however, the town had become a military target, the home of a British garrison preparing to join the retreat to Dunkirk and the English Channel.

In the afternoon, German artillery poured fire on the tower of the library. A witness, an alderman from a nearby town, alleged that a German officer had asked him to identify the library's carillon, and that he later saw the guns of the officer's battery shelling the tower. Other eyewitnesses reported two separate attacks, each lasting perhaps half an hour, which concentrated fire on the library. Tracers (the bright, phosphorescent trails of which allow accurate targeting and spread fire most efficiently) ripped into the building. Tearing through the roof, the shells set fire to books in the attic, which in time burned hot enough to melt the glass flooring of the main gallery. Running down along steampipes, this molten glass spread fire to the manuscript department and rare books room of the cellars; later, it cooled into stalactites that glittered among the shattered stacks. "The whole building," wrote the new rector, Monseigneur Van Waeyenbergh, "was devastated and destroyed." He noted the "awful spectacle of iron beams and metallic framework twisted and turned down, cases of books fallen in with, here and there, pulverized books still in their place." And yet houses and buildings in the vicinity of the library remained standing. The Germans, it appeared, had singled out the library for destruction.

In the days following the attack, the Germans seemed anxious to prove that the fire had been the work of the British. Some witnesses observed the first flames at the library in the early morning before the British withdrawal. The explosion of fire from the cellar stacks finally ripped up the stone floor of the main gallery, which the Germans later pointed to as evidence that the British had placed explosives in the cellar. German newspaper accounts alleged that an expert had found signs of arson in some twelve sites throughout the library. German officers commanding the occupation of Louvain summoned Monseigneur Van Waeyenbergh and a librarian, Professor Etienne Van Cauwenbergh, asking them to certify that stains found on doors were evidence of combustibles used by the English to ignite and accelerate a fire. To both men, the stains looked like varnish that had bubbled, melted, and run in the heat of the flames. The officer who interrogated the librarian in fact asked him to certify that some crates in which a shipment of books had been received— from Japan, no less—were in fact gasoline cans. The librarian later testified that he had rejected their theories; the Germans pressed blame on the British anyway.

Why did the Germans target the library once again? Perhaps they wanted to bring down the tower to prevent its use by Belgian and English snipers or artillery spotters. Indeed, the rector reported (to the Belgian War Crimes Commission, whose report on Louvain's library was published in 1946) that before the German attack the library doorkeeper had found two Belgian soldiers in the tower peering east with binoculars. He told them to leave, arguing that they were uselessly endangering the library (the soldiers' view was not good, he said, and they had no radio or other means of communicating intelligence to superiors). But the Germans never alleged that the tower was an observation post, though they could have justified an attack thereby without resorting to a story about the British.

The 1946 report by the commission supports another explanation. A man named Emile Van Kemmelbeke, whose house outside Louvain was commandeered by Wehrmacht artillery officers, testified as follows:

> [T]hey had a vehicle with them from where they regulated the artillery fire. That vehicle had been put in my garden and I was not allowed to go near it. [Later] they invited me to join them at table. . . . During the meal, a German officer told me that the inscription *Furore Teutonico* was still on the Library. I told him it was not true but the German officers insisted on the contrary.

If this and other eyewitness accounts collected in 1946 by the commission are credible, Wehrmacht officers believed the library to be the monument to the Allied victory—and German disgrace—that the architect Warren and Cardinal Mercier had planned.

The Germans had other reasons to revile Louvain's library. Not only had a new library building risen from the city's ashes, but a new collection as well—and after World War I, Belgian libraries had refilled their stacks with books confiscated from the defeated Germans. The library at Louvain once again held a rich collection, including incunabula and medieval manuscripts; many of these had been taken from the stacks of Germany's own libraries. The officers who spoke to Van Kemmelbeke in his garden that bright and booming May morning, however, made no mention of stolen German books. Yet they believed that among the many unique texts kept in Louvain's library was one they could not abide: a single accusatory line written in stone.

✦

LOUVAIN'S BOOKS were not the only books the Nazis burned, or even the first.

> The whole civilized world was shocked when on the evening of May 10 1933 the books of authors displeasing to the Nazis, including even those of our own Helen Keller, were solemnly burned on the immense Franz Josef Platz between the University of Berlin and the State Opera on Unter den Linden. . . .
>
> All afternoon Nazi raiding parties had gone into public and private libraries, throwing on to the streets such books as Dr. Goebbels in his supreme wisdom had decided were unfit for Nazi Germany.

So reported a shocked Louis P. Lochner, the Berlin correspondent for the Associated Press, from the scene of one of the immense book burnings Nazis staged in the spring of 1933. Lochner saw the bonfires as the public expression of the personality of Josef Goebbels, the leading Nazi intellectual and future culture minister of the new Reich. Goebbels, however, had never ordered the burning of books. The roundup and burning of the books was in fact the work of a pro-Nazi student group, the Deutsche Studentenschaft. The students purged their own libraries and those of their schools, then turned to bookstores and lending libraries for fuel. These last, the *Leih-büchereien*, had long been detested by professional librarians. Found in tobacconists and newspaper stands, they typically consisted of small collections of popular novels: romances, detective stories, and the like. The librarian and Nazi sympathizer Wolfgang Hermann denounced them as "literary bordellos." The book burners would draw on Hermann's wisdom—he had kindly sent them a list of authors—in choosing their fuel. Perhaps Heinrich Heine, whose

Almansor provided a shocked world with an epigraph for the book burnings, was on the list. In their zeal, however, the students and brownshirts had grabbed many books, those of Heine and others, whether they were listed or not.

Although they destroyed the work of dramatists, the book burners did not lack a sense of the dramatic. The burnings were spectacles; as the historian Leonidas Hill points out, "The planners were very conscious of historical precedents, such as the Inquisition's auto-da-fé, Luther's destruction of the papal bulls, . . . and the burning of the Versailles Treaty . . . by Nazi students in 1929." At a book burning in Frankfurt, students rented ox-driven manure carts to carry the books to the site of the bonfires. For safety and civic solemnity, firemen attended the blazes, anticipating one of Ray Bradbury's chief ironies in *Fahrenheit 451*. In this and other innovations, the students who organized the burnings pioneered the aesthetics of the *Thing*-Theater, Nazi-inspired, government-sponsored entertainments that were part of Goebbels's abortive attempt to replace decadent modern drama with theatrical rituals worthy of the *Volk*. As Lochner reported from Berlin, students "performed veritable Indian dances and incantations as the flames began to soar skyward." These incantations, called *Feuersprüche*, or "fire speeches," lent a quasi-religious air to the proceedings; one version went like this:

1. Against class struggle and materialism.
For the national community and an idealistic outlook.
Marx, Kautsky.

2. Against decadence and moral decay.
For discipline and morality in family and state.
H. Mann, Ernst Glaeser, E. Kästner.

3. Against cynicism and political treachery.

For devotion to people and state.

F. W. Förster.

4. Against the debasing exaggeration of man's animal nature.

For the nobility of the human soul.

Freudian school. The Journal *Imago*.

5. Against the falsification of our history and the denigration of
its great figures.

For awe for our past.

Emil Ludwig, Werner Hegemann.

6. Against alien journalism of the democratic-Jewish stamp.

For responsible participation in the work of national
reconstruction.

Theodor Wolff, Georg Bernhard.

7. Against literary betrayal of the soldiers of the World War.

For the education of the nation in the spirit of military
preparedness.

E. M. Remarque.

8. Against the self-opinionated pollution of the German
language.

For the preservation of our nation's most precious possession.

Alfred Kerr.

9. Against arrogance and presumption.

For veneration and respect for the immortal German national
spirit.

Tucholsky, Ossietsky.

Even though Goebbels hadn't written the *Feuersprüche* or organized the burning of books, the ritual delighted him, and he immediately co-opted its energies in the name of the Reich. When word reached him of the burning in Berlin, he rushed over to address the mob in Franz Josef Platz. "German men and women!" Lochner reports him saying. ". . . You are doing the right thing in committing the evil spirit of the past to the flames at this late hour of the night. It is a strong, great and symbolic act, an act that is to bear witness before all the world. . . . Brightened by these flames our vow shall be: The Reich and the Nation and our Führer Adolf Hitler: Heil! Heil! Heil!"

Sigmund Freud, whose name appeared in the *Feuersprüche*, was not impressed. "Only our books?" he reportedly asked. "In earlier times they would have burned us with them." But Freud had evidently forgotten his Heine. This was only the beginning, one of the first of thirty university book burnings in the spring of 1933. Over the course of the next twelve years, one hundred million books (according to one estimate) would accompany six million human beings into the flames of the Holocaust.

As Leonidas Hill has shown, Nazi attacks on culture had begun well in advance of Hitler's giddy rise to power in 1933. Erich Maria Remarque had been an early lightning rod of nationalist frustration; his *All Quiet on the Western Front* was banned in the schools of Thuringia as early as 1929. Across the country, zealots hounded professors from their posts, painted over offensive murals, removed "degenerate art" from museums, and forced the closing of the Bauhaus. In 1930, Thomas Mann's and his daughter's lectures were interrupted, and they, along with Arnold Zweig, Lion Feuchtwanger, and others, endured telephone threats and pursuit by Nazi gangs.

In August 1932, the Nazi newspaper the *Völkischer Beobachter* published a list of writers whose work was to be banned if the Nazis took power. In April 1933, Alfred Rosenberg, the Nazi party's theorist and Goebbels's rival in cultural matters, issued a modest roster of twelve authors. But censorship caught fire, according to Hill; by the end of the Reich's first year, twenty-one separate offices had collectively banned more than a thousand books. A year later, forty agencies joined together in banning some forty-one hundred publications.

For the next few years, Goebbels and Rosenberg competed for the power to ban books and remake German literature in the spirit of the *Volk*. Rosenberg, for all his political power, was only a party official; Goebbels enjoyed the power of the Reich ministries under his command. So where Rosenberg voiced imprecations, Goebbels would issue edicts; and their competitive zeal primed the pump for a torrent of confusing lists and denunciations of literary works. Even as the Reich consolidated under Hitler's leadership, censorship remained the decentralized work of state police units, party mobs, and zealous citizens. Throughout Germany, teachers, students, book-sellers, and librarians were silent as Nazis purged school libraries of banned books. It was up to librarians to replace them with collections tailored to Nazi literary taste.

Even at the height of Nazi censorship in the late thirties and beyond, the Reich's lists of banned books were kept secret. Book-sellers, teachers, and private citizens were left to glean the criteria for exclusion from Goebbels's gnomic pronouncements on the maintenance of the people's spirit. And so it was not only mobs that burned books. Fearing house searches, ordinary Germans burned their own books before the storm troopers could find them. "Those who did try to burn their books," writes Hill, "discovered that this cannot be done easily and quickly. . . . Thick bundles of paper must be separated so that air and flames can consume individual sheets. . . . Otherwise the bundles are only scorched at the edges. . . . Burning large volumes in stoves or fireplaces was tedious and time-consuming."

The Nazis not only burned libraries but built them, too, in their own inimitable fashion. It was as if the destruction of so many books, and the censorship of so much German literature, created a gap that had to be filled—or at least papered over with a simulacrum composed of authentic Nazi literature under strict ideological control. In part, the Nazis worked to transform the disappearing books into capital: as the Reich turned itself into a war machine, the seizing of Jewish booksellers' stores became a source of cash for military buildup, and confiscation of books and manuscripts was joined with the theft of art treasures by which Nazis filled both government coffers and their own purses. The Nazis hoarded books and art, sometimes with the pretense of connoisseurship or intellectual endeavor.

In these efforts, Alfred Rosenberg was most zealous. As his special cultural commandos, the Einsatzstab Reichsleiter Rosenberg (ERR), prowled newly occupied lands in the east, they destroyed great libraries, but stole many outright as well. Hill writes, "In July 1940 Hitler commissioned the Einsatzstab . . . to seize books for the library of a postwar Nazi university, the Hohe Schule. . . . Units of twenty to twenty-five men in special uniforms accompanied the armies in the east, where the ERR investigated 375 archives, 402 museums, 531 institutes, and 957 libraries." Rosenberg's Berlin Ostbücherei contained a million stolen books.

Seizure of Jewish collections swelled the Frankfurt city library's Judaica collection—at the disposal of Rosenberg's Institute for the Study of the Jewish Question—to 550,000 items. "In Poland from December 1939 to March 1940," Hill writes, "the Nazis plundered more than 100 libraries. . . . Estimates range from 600,000 stolen volumes of Judaica and Hebraica from Lodz alone to a million volumes from the entirety of Poland." The Germans "systematically burned" the Krasinski Library, whose underground levels had been sought by Polish librarians as a haven for rare books from the National Library and the University of Warsaw. "In Vilna Dr. Johannes Pohl of the ERR, an expert on Hebrew literature who had studied in Jerusalem, ordered a selection of 20,000 of the choicest volumes from 100,000 collected from several towns and 300 synagogues, and the sale of 80,000 as raw material to a paper-shredding mill." And not only Jewish books were sought. Catholic books, Freemason books, Slavic books—all were ripe for selection. "In Ukraine 150 experts work- ing for the ERR stole or destroyed over 51 million books," Hill writes. ". . . In Belarus more than 200 libraries were plundered; the national library lost 83 percent of its collections, and although 600,000 volumes were later found, 1 million are still missing."

The ERR were also active in the west. After the German occu- pation of Rome in 1943, ERR officers inspected the contents of the Roman synagogue's two great libraries, which contained extraordi- nary collections gathered over the 2,000-year history of Jewish life in Rome. They demanded the libraries' catalogs; just days before the first deportation of Roman Jews to Auschwitz, two specially ordered railcars destined for Rosenberg's institute in Frankfurt were loaded with ten thousand books from the libraries.

Before the war, the public library had been a moribund insti- tution in Germany, where in most respects it remained a repository of elite culture. The historian Margaret Stieg describes prewar librar- ians as divided into two contesting schools known as the Alte Rich- tung and the Neue Richtung, or the Old Way and the New Way. Librarians allied with the Alte—the mainstream segment of librari- anship, in Stieg's estimation—gave a romantic slant to the progres- sive ideals that had animated nineteenth-century librarians elsewhere: they stressed *Bildung*, or personal intellectual and spiritual growth, as the chief use of the library in society. The New Way was the brainchild of Walter Hofmann, a self-educated Leipziger who became the Nazis' chief librarian. To Hofmann, the personal rewards the library offered readers were subordinate to its real purpose: to develop the spirit of the people. As Stieg tells it,

> Where the Alte Richtung looked to England and the United States for inspiration, the Neue Richtung worshipped German-ness. The Alte Richtung stressed the individual, the Neue Richtung thought in collective terms such as "The Public" or "The Bourgeois Housewife." . . . The Alte Richtung saw education as a process, the means by which an individual could achieve full humanity. To the Neue Richtung education was a product, to be purveyed to the library user.

Proponents of the Old Way, finally, saw culture as diverse, manifold, changing; the New Way, however, "held that culture had only one form." Hofmann wanted only "good" books in his library, and classic German works in particular.

When the Nazis came to power, the squabble between Old and New Way was over. Libraries now joined in the great and mystical task of fashioning the German people into a *Volk*. To librarians, the Nazi rise represented a limitless fund of opportunity, and they quickly went to work rebuilding their institutions to aid in the development of the *Volk*. They strove to overcome the Nazi suspicion of books, which Hitler regarded as inferior repositories of inner experience alongside more vigorous and communal forms like architecture. As defined by the Reich, the job of the library would be to control the dangerous, the bourgeois, the effete and dissipating energies of reading, to help the *Volk* find useful information without degrading its "spirit."

Librarians, Stieg says, labored hard to turn the Nazis' ambivalence about reading into useful slogans, to coordinate the library with the Third Reich. Hitler had stated that reading should be "instinctual"—guided by *völkisch* intuition, rather than by educated discrimination. In 1935, German librarians adopted the slogan "the book—a sword of the spirit" for their annual "Book Week" celebrations. The poster for Book Week 1936 quoted the Führer at greater length: "Except for my architecture, the rare visit to an opera, I had books as my only friends. I then read insatiably and fundamentally. In a few years I created the basis of a knowledge on which I still draw." Stieg points out the contradictory energies of this statement: in the Nazi ideal, reading serves a limited purpose; it is but a preliminary stage of life, a necessity to be overcome.

Nonetheless, librarians consolidated their professional position in the new Reich wherever they could, helping to compile lists of authors to censor, eliminating their chief rivals in the small-scale commercial lending libraries, and preemptively purging their own collections of what Goebbels had called "asphalt" literature: all that was modern and obscure. According to Stieg, however, nowhere had libraries laid the groundwork for the Nazi ideals better than in the German-speaking communities of nations outside Germany. Long before National Socialism arose, activists in Czechoslovakia, in Poland, in Alsace and Lorraine, and elsewhere used libraries to foster a sense of ethnicity that was nationalist in orientation. In August 1919—six weeks after the signing of the peace treaty of Versailles—nationalists organized the Grenzbüchereidienst, or Borderland Book Service, to promote libraries and reading rooms in German-speaking communities beyond the borders of the Weimar Republic. Stieg tells that the great promoter of German-language libraries abroad was one Wilhelm Scheffen, a World War I veteran who had started the Society for the Dissemination of Good *Völkisch* Writing. After the rise of the Nazis, the Grenzbüchereidienst was smoothly

integrated into the Reich, and became an important channel for dis-
seminating the ideology of lebensraum and Aryan identity. Thanks
to a generous state support that was absent in the fatherland, German libraries were already strong in Czechoslovakia (a country
whose multiethnic nature a Reich pronouncement called a "disgrace to Europe"), but in the hands of the Grenzbüchereidienst they
became outposts of National Socialism.

Sadly, the Nazi era became a perverse golden age for librarians
in Germany—at least for those who could combine proper ethnic
credentials with an affinity for the Nazis' malignant cultural taste. As
Stieg writes,

> [Librarians] accomplished the redirection of the profession by
> appropriating some of the more pertinent Nazi themes and giv-
> ing them a specifically public library application. The political
> character of the public library was emphasized; the idea of the Volk
> was integrated. . . . Nazi library theory ostentatiously rejected
> Weimar, a rejection that was in fact a repudiation of cultural diver-
> sity and led directly to the purging of collections.

Stieg points out the double bind in which German librarians found
themselves in the Nazi era. "What made this small, rather insignifi-
cant profession"—even more marginal in Germany than elsewhere—"worthy of attention was that librarians were the keepers of
library collections. Librarians acquired, organized, and disseminated
books and other reading material. Nazi determination to dictate
what people read and, more important, what they did not read,
moved librarianship from a peripheral government concern to a
central one." In this regard, librarians had sought "coordination"
actively in the early years of the Reich.

Ultimately, however, libraries proved marginal to Nazis simply because their use was elective. As Stieg shows, the government could not effectively force people to use libraries in the way it could compel the use of other cultural institutions, notably the educational system. And so the Nazis' enthusiasm for books as swords of the spirit waned; the Reich craved not books but bloody swords. Librarians' bargain with Nazism, in the end, was Faustian: only by assuring the Reich of their complacence and marginality did they survive.

BUT IF GERMAN LIBRARIANSHIP barely survived its Faustian bargain with the Nazis, libraries flourished elsewhere, even where Nazi annihilation reigned supreme. As David Shavit writes in *Hunger for the Printed Word*, libraries were part of survival in the ghettos and camps of the Final Solution. In Theresienstadt, the infamous "model Jewish city" the Reich established near Prague, a library of some 100,000 books flourished. Even Block 31 at Birkenau had a library—a sad collection of 8 volumes locked in the block elder's room. And in the Vilna ghetto, amid awful degradation and constant threat of transport to the death camps, Jews built a library. In October 1942, the librarian Herman Kruk prepared a report on the first year of the Vilna ghetto library. An extraordinary document, it now resides in the collection of the YIVO Institute in New York, where it was translated by Zachary M. Baker. It is at once a work of cool library science and a cry of mingled hope and despair.

Dina Abramowicz, who worked for Kruk in the library, wrote about meeting him in the ghetto for the first time:

One evening, stepping out from our crowded quarters into the ghetto street, I bumped into Herman Kruk, the head of the former Grosser Library in Warsaw, an important center of Yiddish secular and socialist cultural activities. Kruk had come with the stream of Jewish refugees from Warsaw. . . . [H]e remained . . . in the hope of returning to Warsaw to rescue his wife from the Nazi clutches. He did not succeed and remained stuck in Vilna. . . .

Kruk remembered Abramowicz from his visits to the children's library, where she had worked. He told her that he had persuaded the Judenrat, the ghetto's Jewish administration, to sponsor the establishment of a new library in the halls of the old one. He explained to her that library workers would be paid by the Judenrat itself, increasing the chance that they would receive work permits necessary to avoid deportation.

Abramowicz joined Kruk's small staff in the freezing halls of the library. They worked constantly, renovating the rooms, taking in books, and cataloging the collection, stopping only in winter when temperatures in the unheated building dipped below freezing. Kruk himself was indefatigable, despite his own hunger and despair. In addition to running the library, he kept a diary that captures painful details of ghetto life. In it, he tells of the concerts and plays staged by Jews desperate for culture; he also unsparingly recounts the torture and deportation of ghetto residents and the harrowing experiences of those who escaped their Lithuanian murderers at Ponary, the nearby execution field in the woods outside Vilna.

But as they struggled with their catalog cards in the library's frigid confines, Kruk and his colleagues caught rare glimpses of repose, and even of joy, among the books. Kruk attempted to document these moments, and the search for them, in his report. His statistics, which he uses to "cast the ghetto reader into bibliopsychological relief," record sundry details: the number of books in the library, the languages of their writing, the number of times they were checked out, and the demographics of their readers. What emerges from these data is a portrait of what reading meant to members of a community exiled to hell.

Kruk notes that as of 1939—before Jews were driven into the ghetto—the principal library of Vilna's Jewish community, the Mefiste Haskalah Library, held a respectable 45,000 books. Kruk notes, "In the first days of September 1941, [this] library lost about 20 percent of its book collections"—and its 40,000-card catalog, too, confiscated by German occupiers, who removed 1,500 volumes in French, English, and German. Another 4,000 volumes went "astray," Kruk notes, when the Jews were driven into the ghetto. No doubt, many were lost with their readers before the vicious German drive. The staff during this time disappeared; the director, Fayvush Krasni, was seized and executed by the Germans in September 1941—one of 19,000 Jews who were shot at Ponary before the ghetto was established. Between October and December 1941, another 33,500 Jews were taken from the ghetto and murdered; barely 20,000 remained alive in Vilna. It was during this hellish time that Kruk cobbled together a staff to "occupy" the library once more, recatalog its contents, and serve readers however they could. For a time, they added volumes to the library in great numbers; in December 1942, the ghetto held a celebration to commemorate an astonishing fact: 100,000 books had circulated since Kruk reopened the library. But Kruk's feelings about his swelling stack were mixed: he records in his diary that the Einsatzstab Reichsleiter Rosenberg was sending him castoff volumes from synagogues and private homes they had raided and destroyed in an effort to "concentrate Jewish books in the Ghetto."

Abramowicz recounts how Kruk's office looked out on the courtyard where the members of the community council had been lined up and shot. A frigid wind whistled through the big hall next door, which Kruk would turn into a new reading room and museum. Soon, Abramowicz writes,

[t]he broken windowpanes were replaced by new ones; the walls were whitewashed with fresh paint. Glass cabinets placed along the walls displayed Torah scrolls, silver wine cups, candle holders, and embroidered curtains for the Torah arks. In the course of time the number of Torah scrolls owned by the museum increased considerably. They arrived in a mysterious way from the surrounding villages, conspicuous signs of disappearing Jewish communities. It was already becoming inadvisable and even impossible to display them all unless one wanted to show that the museum was turning into a graveyard. The scrolls were wrapped in bedsheets and there they lay, silent and hidden, in the corner of the ghetto archives.

By September 1942, Kruk reports that 4,700 subscribers have visited the library. As the collections grew, the library established "branches" in the ghetto prison, the children's home, and elsewhere. Kruk's staff undertook a rigorous recataloging of the library, producing twenty-seven subject catalogs by the time of the report.

In Kruk's report, delightful hand-drawn tables and diagrams depict an array of facts: the composition of the book collection is shown as a shelf of books, with each book standing for a thousand volumes. The types of books lent, too, are shown as books stacked next to each other; an enormous tome represents the 78.3 percent of lent books that were literature; next to it stands a smaller volume representing children's literature (17.7 percent of all loans), and a minuscule book, a miniature, for nonfiction (4 percent). Through these and other tables, Kruk notes telling trends. The proportion of books in Yiddish and Hebrew had increased since the "action" that closed the ghetto. So had the library's readership: 20 percent of all subscribers took books out through the week; on Sunday, the proportion rose to 25 percent.

The books of the library, of course, were not so trim and fresh as those in Kruk's hopeful diagrams. Dina Abramowicz describes the stock of books in the library's care: "[there were] volumes where dozens of pages were missing at the beginning and at the end, and probably no less in the middle, bound and rebound again and again so that the margin was nonexistent and the beginning of the line disappeared somewhere deep in the spine of the book—in short, real invalids of books that had deserved to be retired a long time ago."

But whatever the condition of the book, ghetto residents hungered for them. In a summary section of his report entitled "The Miracle of the Book," Kruk attempts to limn the "psychological attributes" of his readers. "Books," he asks, ". . . for whom could they possibly be of any use now?" He notes that in the early days, when the city "was being drowned in Jewish blood," reading was not only an impossible luxury but a "withdrawal from the surrounding conditions." And yet quite early the ghetto's residents found they couldn't survive without the "narcotic" of the book. Even in the midst of deportation "actions," books circulated—though, as Kruk writes, "[e]ach action . . . left its legacy. Along with the 'borrowed' readers, the books that had been lent to them also departed. Fewer people remained in the ghetto, and fewer books in the library." Kruk continues,

> The ghetto reader is psychologically crippled; his highest ideal is to escape. . . . His minimal concern is that he at the very least will survive. . . . [O]nly two things are possible: reading for the purpose of intoxication—that is, in order to stop thinking—or the contrary, reading in order to ponder, to become interested in comparable fates, to make analogies and reach certain conclusions. . . .
>
> The reader often likes to use a book as a mirror, as a reflection of his situation and the surrounding conditions. . . .

Analogies: It was established that a hungry person reads eagerly about hunger, while someone with a full stomach cannot abide that kind of subject matter.

Here, in ghetto conditions, among a certain stratum of the socially mature intelligentsia, the reading of L. N. Tolstoy (in all available languages)—especially his monumental work *War and Peace*—occupies first place.

Other craved books include the Nazi-banned *All Quiet on the Western Front* and works of Jewish literature and history. Also popular is a history of the massacre of the Armenians at the hands of the Turks. "Who remembers the Armenians?" Hitler once asked his inner circle, reassuring them that ultimately history would ignore the Final Solution, too. But the residents of the ghetto remembered the Armenians.

For the "broad mass" of readers, however, "what suffices is reading matter that removes them from reality. . . . Where one person loses himself through amusement, the other does so by seeking to understand and comprehend." Both impulses, Kruk later allows, are ultimately only "means of escape," and his summary is at once bleak and knowing: "The supply of books is such that we are able to be nourished only by leftovers; nothing new is being, or will be, added. . . . The books are tattered; complete sets are becoming broken sets . . . and soon the library will be left with empty shelves." In September 1943, weeks before the final liquidation of the ghetto, Kruk was deported to Estonia. A year later, he was burned to death in the Kruga concentration camp.

THE LIST OF LIBRARIES DESTROYED in the twentieth century is long. When the People's Liberation Army invaded Tibet, it razed monasteries by the score; hundreds and thousands of books went up in flames. The distinctive form of the Tibetan printed book—long narrow codices printed from wood blocks, clad in saffron covers sewn with crimson thread, a format centuries older than Gutenberg's Bible—nearly ceased to exist. Monks and refugees brought whole libraries over the border to India by horse and mule, where they not only founded new libraries but started new presses, keeping the craft of the Tibetan book, like a lineage of lamas, alive. Elsewhere in China, books suffered terribly during the Cultural Revolution. But everywhere they are read, books burn: in 1981, Sinhalese nationalists torched the Tamil library of Jaffna in Sri Lanka. Home to thousands of manuscripts, palm leaf scrolls, and printed books, it was one of South Asia's greatest repositories of culture and history, a living testament to a multiethnic, ecumenical Sri Lankan society. And three years before the Taliban mined the Buddhas at Bamian, they announced their willingness to destroy culture by burning the 55,000 books of the Hakim Nasser Khosrow Balkhi Cultural Center, in northern Afghanistan, in front of the director's horrified eyes.

Destroying a library, however, is merely the crudest form of editorializing. Libraries left intact can become tools of oppression and genocide, too, since they offer canons that reflect the conceits of mystical nationalism and the will to purity. As Richard Wright relates in what is perhaps the climactic scene in *Black Boy*, his wrenching autobiography, libraries in the Jim Crow South not only deemed some books off-limits; they supported the notion that some people were unsuited to be readers. If the new library offered great progressive hope, so could it deliver unbearable pain in withholding that hope.

Wright's first interest in books, as he tells it, came when as a seventeen-year-old factory worker he came across a newspaper editorial condemning a book by H. L. Mencken. Having already formed an acute appraisal of the oppression found in the South, he determined that if a southern paper disliked what Mencken had written, he must have something worthwhile to say. He wanted to read Mencken. But the library was closed to blacks, and Wright knew that the developmental scheme librarians promoted in the nineteenth century had no room for him.

Perhaps there was a way after all: in the past, he had been permitted entrance in order to pick up books requested by the white men he worked for; now he needed to find someone who was willing to let him say he was picking up books for him, when in fact he would be getting them for himself. This choice had to be made carefully, for approaching the wrong man could mean violence. Finally, he decided to ask Mr. Falk, a Catholic man who, he had noticed, seethed at the bigotry he himself experienced at the hands of southern Protestants. Reluctantly, the man agreed: Wright could use his card and forge his name on notes requesting books—but only if he accepted full responsibility if he was caught.

Wright's portrayal of the dangers of his library forays makes it clear that he lived in a police state, in which authority was vested in every white person. Even something so seemingly innocuous as ordering books at the library became an interrogation, and his first visit to the library with the borrowed card was harrowing. Although he had visited the library many times before, on "errands for whites," Wright now feared that he would "slip up and betray" himself somehow.

At the desk, he removed his cap and waited for the whites in line to be served, trying to look "as unbookish as possible." Finally, the librarian noticed him. Without speaking, he simply handed her Falk's library card and a forged note listing two books by

Mencken. At first, the librarian was incredulous. Wright reminded her that he had run errands in the library for Mr. Falk before, but she remained uncertain, asked him whether he was actually planning to use the books himself. "Oh, no, ma'am," Wright responded. "I can't read."

She turned away to fetch the books, muttering about Mencken. "I knew now that I had won," Wright recalled. "She was thinking of other things and the race question had gone out of her mind. . . . Finally she came forward with two books in her hand." Wright had crossed the border safely. He walked away with two books that day: Mencken's *A Book of Prefaces* and *Prejudices*.

Wright used the library card as a visa to the world of books. At first, it was the sheer force of expression itself that amazed him—not the words, as he said, but the possibility that people should have the courage to say them at all. But it was in novels, ultimately, that his own sensibility emerged and began to grow. No mere recreative reading, these novels—for in them Wright found the means to remake his world. From Sinclair Lewis, he understood his boss as Elmer Gantry. With Dreiser, he revisited the suffering of his mother, which he had been unable to face until then. "It would have been impossible for me to have told anyone what I derived from these novels, for it was nothing less than a sense of life itself."

But it was a dangerous time for Wright, for his newfound bookishness excited the suspicion of the white men who lorded it over him at work.

"Boy, what are you reading those books for?"
"Oh I don't know, sir."
"That's deep stuff you're reading, boy."
"I'm just killing time, sir."
"You'll addle your brains if you don't watch out."

Wright feared that at any moment his newly extended sensibility might reveal itself, enticing a white man to reach out and cut it short again. He guarded his every word, his face, to hide all trace of his new learning.

There can be no doubt that Wright's reception at the library was typical for his time. Black Americans North and South faced condescension, misunderstanding, and outright hostility in public libraries. "In the Northern States," wrote Arthur Bostwick in 1910, "there is theoretically no discrimination. . . . In spite of this, however, the Negro in the North does not use the library as much as might be expected. . . . It would seem that the race feels instinctively, whether with justice or not, that it is not wanted."

According to Eliza Atkins Gleason's 1941 study *The Southern Negro and the Public Library*, public libraries in the South did not exist for blacks until the early years of the twentieth century. Black colleges often had made their library resources available to the community, and they sometimes trained librarians for public library service. But even in those states most amply furnished with libraries, public accommodation of blacks was nearly nonexistent. Georgia, for instance, had fifty-three libraries in 1936, only five of which served blacks; out of forty-four public libraries in Florida, blacks could use four. In the same year, only one of the nineteen public libraries in Arkansas was open to blacks, a pattern followed in nearly all the southern states: of Alabama's eighteen, two; of Kentucky's sixty-four, fourteen; of Louisiana's sixteen, three; of Mississippi's twenty-two, two. West Virginia stands out, for at this time a state law required libraries receiving public monies to offer full access to blacks. But what kind of service, the study does not say. Only in Texas did the percentage of public libraries serving blacks exceed the black percentage of the population, and in most cases the difference is astonishing: in Mississippi, for instance, blacks made up a full

50.24 percent of the total population, while only 8.11 percent of the state's libraries would admit them.

Of course, African Americans did not always have to forge notes to acquire books. In the South, there were the libraries of the historically black colleges; in the antebellum North, freedmen formed literary societies and subscription libraries, much like those in polite white society, by which they made books available throughout their communities. As the historian Elizabeth McHenry has shown, these social libraries thrived independently of the often paternalistic patronage offered by white abolitionists, and contributed to an African American sense of identity that grew stronger as the nineteenth century progressed.

Ironically, one of the first instances of a southern public library's making books available to blacks occurred in Wright's city of Memphis. Gleason writes that in 1903 "the Cossitt Library of Memphis, Tennessee, entered into an agreement with Lemoyne Institute, a negro school, whereby the school would furnish the room and the Cossitt Library would furnish the librarian and the books. In addition to being a school library, this collection was accessible to all interested Negroes in the city of Memphis and its surrounding district."

SARAJEVO'S TOWN HALL, an astonishing example of Moorish Revival architecture known as the Vijećnica, opened on the banks of the Miljacka River in 1896. "Its mix of imposing masonry and architectural frivolity," Kurt Schork wrote in the *New York Times*, "captured the city's postwar personality." In 1914, Archduke Ferdinand and his wife, Sophia, began their fateful car ride at the Vijećnica; a few minutes later, Gavrilo Princip emerged from the crowd to fire the shot that started World War I. But the building's importance throughout the Yugoslav era rested on its postwar task:

housing the 1.5 million books of the Bosnian National and University Library.

At about ten-thirty on the night of August 25, 1992, the Serb nationalist general Ratko Mladic's guns north of the Sarajevo–Pale Road on the high ground of Mount Trebevic opened fire on the Bosnian National and University Library on the river's opposite bank. Residents of the neighborhood of the Vijećnica reported that the evening's blanket bombardment of the city suddenly gave way to shelling focused on the library. A series of explosions rocked the city as incendiary shells slammed into the roof of the library and fell inside, setting the book stacks on fire.

Many Sarajevans made their way to the library, where they began a furious effort to rescue books from the advancing flames and guide survivors out of the building. One staff member, Aida Buturovic, died in the conflagration. Film taken inside the burning library during the fire shows an inferno raging in the spacious main hall, the air filled with smoke and a snow of drifting, charred pages. As firefighters arrived, they came under attack; soldiers in the hills loosed antiaircraft shells and machine-gun fire that did little damage to the building itself, but cut hoses and firefighters to ribbons. Overnight, Bosnian soldiers pulled books from the library under withering fire from Serb nationalist positions. Rescue efforts continued over the next several days; a fire brigade commander later remembered watching books fly through the air above the library. Onlookers described ash and paper from the library fire filling their courtyard. One Sarajevan told the reporter Kurt Schork that "even on fire the building is very beautiful." The Bosnian poet Goran Simic gathered bits of burned paper as they fluttered down; he later wrote a poem, "Lament for Vijećnica," which expresses the tragic absurdity of the library's destruction. "Set free from the stacks," he wrote, "characters wandered the streets / mingling with passers-by and the souls of dead soldiers."

The story of Nikola Koljevic, a onetime scholar who rose through the ranks of the nationalist Serb government, tells much about the interwoven motives and resentments that drove the library's destroyers. Before the war, Koljevic had been a noted authority on Shakespeare. Along with his scholarship, he wrote poetry and criticism, and he thrived in the cosmopolitan milieu of Sarajevo. In a story written for the *Manchester Guardian* in March 1997, the reporter Janine Di Giovanni described how Koljevic turned away from scholarship to embrace Serbian nationalism, rising to become vice-president of the Bosnian Serbs and "Iago to Othello, whispering in [Radovan] Karadzic's ear."

Nikola was not the only notable Koljevic in Sarajevo. His brother Svetozar, an authority on American literature, was beloved by his students and better known than Nikola. In addition, Svetozar, whose wife was a Bosnian of Muslim origin, was more at home in the multicultural lifestyle of a Yugoslav intellectual. When Nikola's son died in a skiing accident in the late seventies, Koljevic descended into a depression that led him to turn to Serbian nationalism and orthodox mysticism. He became an early disciple of the Nationalist Serb leader Radovan Karadzic (who had poetic pretensions himself); with his refined manners and his fluent English, he became an important spokesperson for the cause and quickly gained power. Fleeing with Karadzic to the nearby resort town of Pale in 1992 to set up a Bosnian Serb capital, Nikola Koljevic directed the siege of Sarajevo. To him, it was the Vijećnica that represented everything he hated about the city: it contained its diverse history and embodied its Ottoman legacy; within its walls the scholarly life, which ultimately had attracted Svetozar but alienated Nikola, thrived. According to Di Giovanni's account, in the end it was Nikola—a former scholar who over many years had made extensive use of the Bosnian National and University Library— who signed the directive ordering Ratko Mladic to shell the Vijećnica and destroy the library.

Di Giovanni filed her story some six weeks after Nikola Kolje-vic shot himself. The former vice-president had his reasons: definitely excluded from political power, humiliated by the Dayton accords that ended both the war and the nationalist aspirations of the Bosnian Serbs, he was biding his time, awaiting indictment for war crimes. To acquaintances and colleagues interviewed by Di Giovanni, people whose lives were torn apart by his policies, Koljevic's destruction of the library must have counted among the reasons for his suicide as well. One acquaintance, a scholar who was forced to use his own books for fuel during Sarajevo's long siege, told Di Giovanni about an essay Koljevic had written about Macbeth. "In an attempt to become more than he is, Macbeth virtually destroys himself," Nikola had observed. The scholar paused to reflect. "That sentence," he continued, "can beautifully serve as an epitaph on Nikola's grave."

The Vijećnica was not the only library the Serbs attacked; its destruction was just one instance in a campaign carried out against Bosnian lettered culture. Three months earlier, Serb nationalists had attacked the Oriental Institute with incendiary grenades; the losses, described by the librarian, scholar, and activist András Riedlmayer, included 5,263 bound manuscripts in Arabic, Persian, Hebrew, and *adzamijski* (Bosnian Slavic written in Arabic script); 7,000 Ottoman documents, primary source material for five centuries of Bosnia's history; a collection of nineteenth-century cadastral registers; and 200,000 other documents of the Ottoman era. The Bosnian National Museum and National Archives of Herzegovina were also shelled, as were the library of the University of Mostar, the Museum of Herzegovina, the Roman Catholic diocesan library of Mostar

(50,000 books lost), and, as Riedlmayer has documented, hundreds of other libraries, museums, and architectural treasures throughout Croatia, Bosnia, Herzegovina, and, more recently, Kosovo. In this record of destruction, however, the National and University Library of Bosnia represents perhaps the greatest loss; most of its 1.5 million volumes, including over 150,000 rare books, were destroyed. Jeffrey Spurr, Riedlmayer's colleague and the coordinator of a multinational effort to rebuild Bosnia's irreplaceable collections, calls it "arguably the worst single case of deliberate book burning in history in absolute terms." Spurr notes that the library "enshrined the strivings of generations," that the works it contained showed that despite the arguments of Serb nationalists and Western critics alike, "multi-confessional Bosnia had thrived under centuries of Ottoman rule and then decades of Austrian and Yugoslav rule, its inhabitants of whatever background able not simply to live next to but also with each other." And for that very reason it became a target for the guns of the nationalists.

To Riedlmayer, too, the nationalists' motive is all too apparent. "Throughout Bosnia," he has written, "libraries, archives, museums and cultural institutions have been targeted for destruction, in an attempt to eliminate the material evidence—books, documents and works of art—that could remind future generations that people of different ethnic and religious traditions once shared a common heritage. . . ." Riedlmayer has written eloquently about *Convivencia*, the animating notion of the culture of Moorish Spain, in which the traditions of Muslims, Jews, and Christians were understood to contribute to a civilization greater than the sum of its parts. Similar notions, Riedlmayer argues, once animated the intellectual and cultural life of the Balkans in the Ottoman era. But the Serb nationalists who besieged Sarajevo in August 1992 could not abide so direct a contradiction of the cherished ideals of ethnic purity. "What's odd in all this," Riedlmayer has written, "is the reversal of perspectives— the 'ethnic cleansers' show a keen understanding of cultural and religious factors: these are the main criteria on which they select their targets." Their attempted destruction of Bosnian libraries is cruelly ironic, because it confirms Western prejudices about the intractable mutual hatreds prevalent in the Balkans, even as it erases the very evidence of its contradiction: the rich and varied products of a millennium of cultural and intellectual conviviality in the region. Western peacekeepers, aid workers, and bureaucrats, meanwhile, fail to acknowledge cultural destruction for the harbinger of genocide that it is.

When András Riedlmayer was a child, his family fled the communist takeover of Hungary. Now he is a librarian and a historian whose specialty is Islamic southern Europe. His office in Harvard's Fine Arts Library is a quiet, brightly lit space stuffed with books, binders, and overflowing file boxes. In this office, Riedlmayer and Jeffrey Spurr run the library's Islamic art program and direct a host of projects dedicated to the preservation of Balkan civilization and efforts to bring those who would destroy it to justice. His files hold evidence of war crimes: photographs, witness statements, field notes, and reports documenting the destruction of cultural monuments from Bosnia to Kosovo. Atop a cabinet lie a few covered petri dishes, which also hold evidence: charred remains of the burned books of which András has made himself custodian. The first time I visited him in his office, it occurred to me that András is a librarian of burned books.

Like fragments from the Villa of the Papyri at Herculaneum, these cinders bear fragmentary evidence of their origin: on some, the ghosts of letters are visible, blacker than the ashen paper. Larger chunks often consist of fused pages, the edges of which fan in the delicate, telltale manner of a book's fore edge. "It turns out that it's actually very hard to burn books," András tells me with a smile, echoing the bitter lessons frightened German book owners learned when the Nazis came to power. He shows me pictures taken inside shattered mosques in Kosovo: charred books piled waist-high in corners, where they had been doused with gasoline and torched. "The pages of a book are pressed tightly together, which makes it hard for oxygen to feed the fire," András reminds me. "The attackers did not realize this." Many of the books in these photos are beyond repair, and yet retain their shape, and blocks of text are plainly visible in the jumble. Still more, though damaged, could be cleaned and read once again.

The Bosnian Manuscript Ingathering Project searches libraries around the world to locate copies of materials lost during the war in Bosnia, while the Bosniaca Bibliographic Database, built by a broad consortium of university libraries, compiles a bibliography of lost Bosnian materials as the first step in rebuilding a national collection. At the same time, Riedlmayer is also building a database to document the destruction of libraries and cultural monuments in the Balkans for evidentiary use in future war crimes trials. Most recently, he traveled to The Hague to testify in the war crimes trial of the former Serb president Slobodan Milosevic.

Over coffee one afternoon in the summer of 2001, András reminded me of another way to burn books, explained to him by a colleague who survived the siege of Sarajevo. In the winter, the scholar and his wife ran out of firewood, and so began to burn their books for heat and cooking. "This forces one to think critically," András remembered his friend saying. "One must prioritize. First, you burn old college textbooks, which you haven't read in thirty years. Then there are the duplicates. But eventually, you're forced to make tougher choices. Who burns today: Dostoevsky or Proust?" I asked András if his friend had any books left when the war was over. "Oh yes," he replied, his face lit by a flickering smile. "He still had many books. Sometimes, he told me, you look at the books and just choose to go hungry."

CHAPTER SEVEN

Lost in the Stacks

Once upon a time, a boy climbed a ladder and gazed through a window toward the far-off desert outside Cairo. He looked up: at the high end of the ladder, a small hole gaped in the wall. He looked down: the papers clutched in his hand were crumpled and sweaty. They were pages from exercise books, random notes and letters, refuse; his task was to ascend the tall ladder and poke the wad of paper through the hole.

Finally he arrived at the top, trembling and out of breath. He stared at the hole, which was as dark as a mouth. This was the geniza, the grave of written things—any page of which, the rabbi told him, may contain the name of God. This is where books go when they die. His face taut, the boy gulped down his sudden fear and jammed the wadded leaves into the hole. He forced them through at last with a single finger, jabbing quickly to keep it out of the dark. The papers fell out of sight, disappearing with a faint rustle somewhere below.

The boy retreated down the rattling ladder to solid earth, away from this graveyard in the air to the safety of unbroken prayer books and fresh, blank sheets of papyrus.

Geniza: the word in Hebrew means "container." In the rabbinical tradition, it comes to signify a kind of book tomb, a place in the synagogue where writings of all sorts are put when they are worn out. All the tattered pages—whether from liturgical poems or old Haggadahs or children's copybooks—are gathered and put in a geniza for safekeeping, until they can be given a proper burial. The great rabbinical scholar Solomon Schechter described it this way: "When the spirit is gone, we put the corpse out of sight to protect it from abuse. In like manner, when the writing is worn out, we hide the book to preserve it from profanation. The contents of the book go up to heaven like the soul."

Veneration of the written word is common to the peoples of the Book. The Koran, like the Torah, is too holy simply to be discarded; Allah's book is an aspect of his personality. Chiltan Mountain near Quetta, Pakistan, is laced with caves that contain some fifty thousand buried Korans, each one shrouded, like the dead, in white cloth. The mountain is a pilgrimage site for Muslims throughout Asia; many caves have been turned into prayer rooms where the pious keep vigil among the stacked and shrouded pages. It is said that those who are buried near the mountain—popularly called the Mountain of the Holy Korans—are forgiven their sins.

This Islamic practice is not new. Workers restoring Yemen's Great Mosque at Sana'a in 1972 discovered a huge rotting pile of manuscripts, which they stuffed into sacks and set aside. Among the tattered leaves, scholars later discovered pages of Koranic text dating from the first two hundred years of Islam. Intriguingly, some contained variants of the standard version accepted today, offering tantalizing clues regarding the textual history of Islam's holy book.

The Jewish geniza, however, recognizes the sacral quality not of a single book (shredded or whole) but of the written word in general. As a result, abandoned and forgotten genizas have long been important sources of manuscript Judaica. But the geniza of Cairo's synagogue was uniquely long-lived: out of the way, accessible only by ladder, its books, letters, and sundry papers piled up, mingled, and moldered for a thousand years, from the ninth century A.D. until the nineteenth.

In 1890, the synagogue was renovated, and large amounts of material streamed from the geniza into the markets, where they found their way into the acquisitive hands of European travelers. In 1896, two Scottish women, Agnes Lewis Smith and Margaret Dunlop Gibson, having purchased odd bits of manuscripts while touring Cairo, upon their return to England gave Solomon Schechter two fragments of Hebrew writing. Schechter, then a professor at Cambridge, discovered that one fragment belonged to the Book of Ben Sira (Ecclesiasticus), the text of which had previously been known only in Greek. The book was written in about 200 B.C.; the original Hebrew version had been lost for a millennium.

Spurred by this discovery, Schechter made a trip to Cairo, where he obtained permission to take away whatever he wished from the geniza. Schechter's description of the state of the geniza is evocative, and worth quoting at length:

One can hardly realize the confusion . . . until one has seen it. It is a battlefield of books, and the literary productions of many centuries had their share in the battle, and their *disjecta membra* are now strewn over its area. Some of the belligerents have perished outright, and are literally ground to dust in the terrible struggle for space, whilst others, as if overtaken by a general crush, are squeezed into big, unshapely lumps, which even with the aid of chemical appliances can no longer be separated without serious damage to their constituents.

Overwhelmed by the splendor and decay, Schechter decided to restrict his acquisitions to manuscripts, leaving out some four hundred years' worth of printed items. Scholars rue that choice now; since Schechter's time, great interest has grown around the history of printed Judaica. In any event, Schechter's inventory is awesome; it comprises some 100,000 fragments in all, including biblical texts, phylacteries, Apocrypha and Pseudepigripha, Mishna, Talmud texts by Maimonides and others, liturgical poetry, letters, bills, lists, amulets, calendars, catalogs, children's exercises and readers, dictionaries, illuminations, charms, cabalistic texts, medical texts, names, polemics, poetry, vocabularies, Arabic children's writing, Arabic grammars, histories, scientific texts, and Arabic Judaica.

In the years since Schechter first described the contents of the Cairo geniza, they have gradually been dispersed on both sides of the Atlantic. The bulk of the fragments reside in New York's Jewish Theological Seminary and at Cambridge University. But they've been brought together again in the scholarship of S. D. Goitein, whose six-volume study of them, *A Mediterranean Society*, gives an extraordinary account of Jewish life in the Middle Ages, showing connections among the economic, political, ethnic, intellectual, and personal spheres of the Judeo-Islamic world.

So is the geniza a library? In the strict sense of the term, of course, it is not. Libraries offer access, and the geniza was for many centuries inaccessible. Moreover, the library's books are chosen and approved, deemed worthy of preservation. And in this the geniza is the library's opposite: its contents were the things thrown out, discarded specifically for their uselessness. In a more fundamental sense, however, the geniza *is* a library—for libraries collect and store books for future use, and this the geniza certainly has done; in its collection and preservation of unique cultural artifacts it is unparalleled among the libraries of the world. It could be said that the geniza preserved its materials better than a library would have done. For while its fragments were undoubtedly harmed by inattention, they fared better over their long incarceration than books do in even the most conservation-minded libraries, where they are subject to handling, movement, loss, attack, and theft. More interestingly, the fact that they were deemed valueless is precisely what makes them invaluable to us today. They convey a far more comprehensive message from their times than any vetted and authorized library collection ever could. It's their throwaway, quotidian aspect—forcefully evoked by Schechter in the passage above, which evokes as well the battle-of-the-books metaphor of Jonathan Swift—that makes them such a powerful testimonial to the beauties of people otherwise forgotten.

The geniza has no ax to grind, ideological or otherwise. This above all makes it the library's opposite, for regardless of the library's alleged political neutrality, its transparency, its seeming lack of roots, it contains the buried and often contradictory impulses of the princes, philanthropists, and academicians who are its authors. Alexander, after all, meant his library to corner the ancient market in intellectual capital; Dewey wanted a library that not only operated efficiently but promoted efficiency in readers' lives. Unlike these libraries—conditional, ideological, argumentative—the geniza is a simple refuse pile, unafraid of its own collected contradictions.

IN THE WAINSCOTED, SUN-WASHED HALL of a Wisconsin farmhouse, centuries after the ladder to Cairo's geniza toppled, a set of books sits atop a lace-covered table. Perhaps twenty volumes are snugly tucked into a portable bookcase built, like the *armaria* of ancient Rome, with two doors flung open wide to reveal a double set of tiered shelves. Twenty books in a little cupboard; that is all. And yet the image of them, reproduced in Arthur Bostwick's *The American Public Library*, shows that even in a few gathered volumes the aura of the library may reside. These books are an example of what librarians at the turn of the century called a "home library"—not a privately owned collection, but a set of books gathered together and sent out to readers in the countryside. An early version of the bookmobile, the home library traveled to the farmsteads of rural Wisconsin in a horse-drawn, librarian-driven buggy. It's modest, and even homely, set down beneath an obscure portrait, framed by two simple black chairs. Yet there's a bit of Alexandria contained in that cupboard of books—a whiff of the Vatican, the Sorbonne, the Round Reading Room, the granite majesty of the Boston Public Library. The sturdy bindings of the home library seem to shed light into the farmhouse room. Arranged on the shelves of the bookcase they make a diptych, an altar filling the room with the glow of books.

Bostwick describes two kinds of home libraries. In addition to the collections circulated to rural readers, another sort of minilibrary was offered in the urban setting, especially to children of immigrants. In the city, Bostwick relates, a librarian or volunteer would go into the neighborhoods with these collections and look for a child to whom she could confidently lend them. The hope was that the child would not only read the books herself but share them with family and friends. In a week or so, the librarian would return to the tenements to collect the books, discuss them with the children, and offer another collection for them to borrow.

The combination of settlement-house outreach and library science was a product of the twentieth century designed to further nineteenth-century goals: to bring untutored masses into the circle of readers, to set them on a path to right reading that would lead from adventure stories and travel tales to geography, history, and the trades. The expectation was that enjoyment of the home library would entice young readers into the children's room of the local branch, where they would begin the process of inculcation to the values of their society.

And yet in some cases, these immigrant children took the library books they were offered and used them to fashion a new world, a new America all their own. For them, the recreational reading that nineteenth-century librarians scorned—in particular the reading of novels—became the real work of the library. Libraries figure prominently in the work of Mary Antin and Alfred Kazin—both of whose families emigrated from Russia's Pale of Settlement (the only lands in which the czars permitted Jews to reside) around the turn of the twentieth century. Both writers reimagine the library in ways that support and subvert the ideals of an earlier generation.

It is her partial ownership of the public library that most effectively symbolizes for Antin the rights her new society grants her. In her often breathless memoir *The Promised Land*, she calls the Boston Public Library "one of my favorite palaces." She watches visitors throng the library: "children [who] hushed their chatter at the entrance, . . . patting the great stone lions at the top" of the grand stairs. She watches "spectacled scholars . . . loaded with books," who are unaware of their own echoing steps. And tourists, too, who "lingered long in the entrance hall, studying the inscriptions and symbols. . . . All these eager children, all these fine-browed women, all these scholars going home to write learned books—I and they had this glorious thing in common, this noble treasure house of learning. It was wonderful to say, *This is mine;* it was thrilling to say, *This is ours.*" At the end of the "vast reading room" of Bates Hall, Antin

The home library, from Bostwick's The American Public Library *(New York: Appleton, 1910). Widener Library B 7739.10 (copy B).*

felt the "grand spaces under the soaring arches as a personal attribute of my being." The library is more to Antin than a hallowed repository of civilization; it contains all the energies of a new home she felt entitled to call her own without reservation or apologies—only with gratitude. "That I who was brought up to my teens almost without a book should be set down in the midst of all the books that were ever written was a miracle as great as any on record."

Assimilation was among the goals of the public library, of course, but Antin's onrushing spirit of ownership and involvement— this went beyond anything the library pioneers might have envisioned. (Certainly it went beyond the wishes of Melvil Dewey—a bigot who hid his antisemitism under the cloak of sober administration, barring Jews from the summer resort he founded in upstate New York.) To library leaders of the nineteenth century, the library

Bates Hall in the Boston Public Library as Mary Antin knew it.
In Bostwick's The American Public Library *(New York: Apple-*
ton, 1910). Widener Library B 7739.10 (copy B).

was an engine or a factory for producing *efficient* readers—people
who read usefully, ignored the frivolity and dross of literature, and
used books to advance themselves and their society. Such practical
notions departed radically from the ideal of previous generations, in
which the library was a treasure house, a cabinet of wonders, a
chicken coop of the muses. The library, the reform-minded thought,
should be progressive, purposive, and proletarian. The masses should
leave the library better prepared to pursue trades, save money, and
stay sober. Emancipation or individual enlightenment was at most a
secondary goal. But the library, especially the large public library
with its endless supply of books, offered more possibilities than the
ideals of philanthropists and administrators.

Like Antin, Alfred Kazin was blissfully unaware of the modest, practical uses the founders of the public library movement intended him to make of books. In the heart of the Great Depression, Kazin fashioned himself into an intellectual amid the hum and rustle of the New York Public Library. "For almost five years," he writes in *New York Jew*,

I had worked . . . in the great open reading room, 315, of the New York Public Library, often in great all-day bouts of reading. . . . Year after year I seemed to have nothing more delightful to do than to sit much of the day and many an evening at one of those great golden tables acquainting myself with every side of my subject. Whenever I was free to read, the great Library seemed free to receive me.

In the passage that follows, Kazin builds a metaphor: the library as America, as *his* America of dreamers and doers. In room 315, he encounters (in the person of their books and columns) the publishers, newspapermen, and writers who have hewn literary modernism out of the rough and tumble of the nineteenth century. Their vivid shades stream past him as a mobile crowd: Eugene Debs, Max Eastman, Upton Sinclair, H. L. Mencken, Edmund Wilson, Theodore Dreiser, Allen Tate, and all the nameless hucksters and night owls of Chicago. They're a surging mob, this bunch—hands in their pockets, hats pulled low—and Kazin roams among them like a flâneur of the mind.

Kazin is an idler; the library doesn't care. "I was my own staff researcher, a totally unaffiliated free lance and occasional evening college instructor who was educating himself in the mind of modern America by writing. . . ." Here he is, the American reader at his self-sufficient best.

No one behind the information desk ever asked me *why* I needed to look at the yellowing, crumbling, fast-fading material about insurgent young Chicago and San Francisco publishing houses in 1897. No one suggested I might manage whatever-it-was-I-was-doing with something more readily available than the very first issue of *Poetry* in 1912; *The New Republic* in 1914; muckraking *Collier's* in the Theodore Roosevelt era;

and a host of other buried signals in the current of emergent American literary modernism. Kazin succumbs to the dream of the research library, a dream not unlike the rags-to-riches fantasies of the penny dreadfuls—the dream of a personal success unaided by unnamed others. Like most readers, Kazin believes that the stuff he wants has been lost here, forgotten, discarded—that the library is a geniza that offers up its secrets only to the most indefatigable scholars. Of course, someone acquired these yellowing, fading materials; of course, someone cataloged them; of course, someone retrieved them from the shelves and will return them when the reader is finished. But in the library these assistants hide behind the curtains; the library becomes a stage with a mirror for a backdrop that reflects only the reader and obscures the multifarious origins of the books.

Libraries of a century before displayed their books as objects of veneration. The new libraries of the early twentieth century, however, hid away the books, rendering them accessible only by staff employing the latest technology: telephones, conveyor belts, elevators. The cover of the May 27, 1911, issue of *Scientific American* showed a cutaway view of the stacks of the New York Public Library, then newly opened. The view shows the all-male staff bustling among the shelves below floor level, sending volumes to the delivery room via a complex network of shafts and booklifts.

Beyond the delivery room windows sit the blissfully browsing readers, unaware of the machinery employed to bring them their reading material.

But for all the technological complexity of New York's new
library building, the author of the *Scientific American* article was more
impressed with the library's efficient handling of people. "The
necessity of supplying books for all classes of readers," he wrote,
"rendered it advisable to devise an architectural plan and an execu-
tive system which would distribute the reader rather than the volumes which he reads." The author's emphasis on "classes of readers"
mirrors the concerns of the nineteenth-century public library pioneers. He concludes by noting that the architects have designed a
library "which is not only a work of art in itself and a worthy monument to the largest city in the western hemisphere, but which
automatically, we may say, divides the thousands of readers who wish
to consult the books *into the intellectual classes in which they belong*" (my
emphasis).

Unaware of the goals of efficient administration, readers like
Kazin rearrange as they see fit both themselves and the books they
read. "Years before I saw Chicago," Kazin writes, "I learned what
hope, élan, intellectual freshness came with those pioneer realists out
of the Middle West. . . ." Kazin finds his Midwest in the library, too—
an idealized "Middle West" of clear-eyed creators, madmen in shirt-
sleeves, visored visionaries "who said there was no American
literature but the one *they* were rushing to create." The library contains it all: the city's creative anonymity, the frumpery and finery of
the gilded age, the archaeology and geography of Manhattan, and,
above all, the American people themselves, brought together in what
Kazin calls "that asylum and church of the unemployed; of crazy ide-
ologists and equally crazy Bible students doggedly writing 'you lie!'
in the reference books on the open shelves; of puzzle fans searching

The library as factory: efficient administration of books, staff, and readers in the New York Public Library as depicted on the cover of the May 27, 1911, issue of Scientific American.

every encyclopedia; of commission salesmen secretly tearing address lists out of city directories." Everyone in Kazin's library is haunted, as desperate as Enoch Soames lost in his own diabolical future. This is a new archetype for the library, one far removed from its previous guiding images—bookworms buzzing in the cage of the muses; a solitary Saint Jerome in his carrel with his lion and his skull; the factory or the marketplace of commonsense ideas. And yet, for all its newness, Kazin's idea of the library connects seamlessly with those that came before it. To Kazin, writing on the eve of the war in which one hundred million books would burn, the library is a crucible of urban civilization, its quintessence.

For Kazin's parents, the object called the book was sacred, singular, and rare. Its type set by God, it could be said (in its first form, the Torah) to be the chief object in the world. And it was awfully expensive. That was the book for his parents' generation—a seventeenth-century conception of the book, though it was held throughout the West well into the twentieth century. But suddenly Kazin and his contemporaries found they could immerse themselves in stacks of books, that there was no end to the books they could have "just for the asking." Kazin, like Antin before him, powerfully reimagined the institution of the library. If the home library can be an altar and a viral speck of civilization, if a few books in a wooden box could open like the ark on a farmstead in Wisconsin, what could massed millions of books—all just sitting there waiting—do for immigrants and their children lost among the shifting crowds of New York, Boston, Chicago?

OTHERS HAVE CHOSEN THEIR BOOKS in the face of hunger and cold. Walter Benjamin, for one, risked his life for a single book—and an unfinished one, at that. But long before he packed the manuscript of his monumental *Arcades Project* under his arm and fled over the Pyrenees to escape the advancing fascists, Benjamin pondered the idiosyncrasies that every reader expresses in his own collection of books. In the essay "Unpacking My Library," Benjamin delights in his books as objects. Taking them from boxes, making room for them on shelves, he discovers their true life as material things—the point at which they are free to take on lives of their own. "To a book collector," he writes, "the true freedom of all books is somewhere on his shelves." The universality of books is reflected darkly; it is their individuality that comes to the fore.

Readers have always opposed the manic energies of the universal library with the hope that one book could explain all. The yearning for such a book, which begins with the Bible, has always been part of the culture of letters. But Benjamin finds that any humble book, in its relation to its owner, may become the Book of Fate. So the personal library carries with it a potential that the publicly owned collection or the academic library, as Benjamin points out, tends to obscure. As the library offers passage into the universe of possible ideas, so the book as cherished object reveals to its owner the connections that individual books can make across time and place, reflected in the story of its previous owners, the history of its bindings, its uncut pages. The book is a tool, and like all tools, it tells the story of its making. It is the door and the key, the passport and the transport. How tragic, then, that Benjamin ended his own life carrying his unfinished book—the manuscript of *Das Passagen-Werk*, a library in and of itself—to safety and liberty. The book became in Benjamin's final days an anchor, a boulder to push up the mountainside, a world borne along on his hunched and bookish shoulders. If it was a burden, however, then he carried it happily. Ultimately, that one object's aura glowed most brightly on the stage that was Benjamin himself. "This book is more important than I am," he told his companions on his final, abortive trek over the Pyrenees.

✦

MUCH HAS CHANGED among the massed millions of books in Widener Library since the first time I lost myself in the stacks. Like those of all lovers of libraries, my bibliographical reveries are not enough to stop time. Today, Widener is in the final throes of a thorough renovation; the stairway I descend is freshly painted and new, its smell faintly fungal. The green, tubular handrails chime as I slide my ring finger along them. The *Lingo Language Games* and the brittle paper of the X-cage are now long gone, moved to off-site storage. It's harder now to find older books in the stacks, the rebound incunabula and vellum-clad eighteenth-century folios having been moved to safer quarters.

Where will I find the book you are now reading? Its place in the library is determined by anonymous others: first, the librarians who draw up the cataloging classifications of the Library of Congress. The process is dizzying in its distribution, offering endless opportunities for differing interpretations and outright errors. The LC subject classes—those nesting, cross-referenceable rubrics ("United States—Social Conditions—to 1865") that once ordered the subject card catalogs and that online users still search in the distributed databases—make up an epistemological labyrinth unto themselves.

And not everyone is happy with them. In seeking a lofty common denominator, useful for libraries of all shapes, sizes, and specialties, the Library of Congress subject classes often strike a tone of bureaucratic high-handedness. Sanford Berman, a librarian in Minnesota's Hennepin County Library since 1973, has waged a battle against subject headings he considers racist, reactionary, insulting to human dignity, and plain confusing. In the process, he and a merry band of fellow catalogers turned the HCL catalog into an exemplary tool for readers.

Even a partial list of the substitutions Berman and colleagues have made is at once comical and telling: where LC has the evasive, but etymologically correct, "amicide," Berman offers the plainer term "friendly fire casualties"; he would replace the impressive "dysmenorrhea" with a frank "menstrual cramps." But the difference between Berman's cataloging style and that of LC is more than ideological: his cataloging is artisanal. Where librarians are generally pressed to accept ready-made catalog records, gathered in astronomical numbers by consortiums and made available to subscribing libraries over computer networks, Berman insists on using his own intelligence to describe each book the library acquires. Thus, his records often contain added information, such as tables of contents and detailed descriptive notes, which are enormously helpful to the reader trying to determine, for example, whether Ntozake Shange's *Whitewash* is a work exploring the impact of a racist hate crime, or a how-to book about house painting.

Library administrators from Melvil Dewey to the present have argued that such hands-on work slows down the process at the heart of the library's mission: putting books into readers' hands. But to Berman, the top-down, networked library fails on its own terms. The reader isn't guided efficiently to the right resource; instead, she is alienated and confused by subject classes that emphasize professional knowledge. The efficiencies produced are largely those beneficial to the administrators of large library networks.

Those efficiencies now seem poised to win out. Berman was forced into early retirement—a fate his catalog will share in the wake of its planned replacement with a streamlined, standardized database. When librarians around the country protested the scuttling of the Berman catalog, however, administrators thought twice. It now appears that the catalog will find a home, possibly in the archives of a library school or the American Library Association itself. This is good news for specialists, but cold comfort for the readers of Hennepin County.

My book, perhaps, doesn't need elaborate or controversial subject headings. And yet I wonder: will catalogers classify my book as history, memoir, or fiction? Will they send it to the GT class, which includes works on "customs and manners, including eating and drinking"? More likely, I'll find it in the Ps, reserved for language and literature. But what about the C class, which contains the "Auxiliary Sciences of History"—in particular CD, for emblems, seals, and archives? Despite all the arguable choices, I'm fairly certain that I will find my book in the Bibliography classification, which the catalogers in their modesty have tucked in at the end of the alphabet: the Z class, which holds the following: "Books (General). Writing. Paleography. Book industries and trade. Libraries. Bibliography." Yes, definitely the Zs. And so, nearly at the bottom of the Widener East Stack stairway, I stop at C level, home of the Z class. "No Roof Access," a sign on the door warns me.

Differentiations abound, however; the Z class, like the rest, is divided by a mixture of rationality, prejudice, and whim. Where to turn? I've written an inoffensive book, I think, unlikely to show up in Z1019–1033, where "prohibited books" are classed. And although it contains the traces of all my reading, it's no personal bibliography, found at the very end of the classification, Z8001–8999. Then there are "Libraries in relation to special topics," Z716.2–718.8; Z702, "thefts and losses of books"; Z102–104.5, "Cryptography. Ciphers. Invisible Writing." I'd like to think it might find its way into the part of the class reserved for "Best Books." But that's Z1035–1035.9—a mere nine-tenths' worth of space. Probably not enough room.

Here is Z719–725, in the spacious zone reserved for books about "Libraries (General)." I turn down this range of shelves. The incandescent bulbs that once punctuated these rows with a faint ocher light are gone, replaced by the diffuse, tidy glow of fluorescent tubing. Pipes gleam overhead; they carry water at high pressure, primed to erupt at the first whiff of smoke or heat and douse the flaming books. No flames today, fortunately, despite the frequent fire alarms that break up the week for Widener readers and staff (dust from renovation and construction trips the alarms regularly). The Z class and its neighbors are among those least frequently visited by readers, and the sound of my footfalls on the marble is joined only by the nearly subliminal buzz of the lighting above me.

Here I am: the Z721s. What else is here? I see a few suggestive titles: *The Happy Bookers: A Playful History of Librarians and Their World from the Stone Age to the Distant Future*, by Richard Armour; *The Care of Books: An Essay on the Development of Libraries and Their Fittings, from the Earliest Times to the End of the Eighteenth Century*, by John Willis Clark; *Grundzüge der Bibliotheksgeschichte*, by one Joris Vorstius; *The First 350 Years of the Harvard University Library*, by my mentor Kenneth Carpenter. The bindings are myriad, endless variations in buckram. I run my finger along them, making a dry rhythmic hiss against the grain of stiff fabric. But my own book is missing. I stoop to ankle level, to where it should be shelved. All I find is a little tent of darkness—an empty space, a geniza hole—where the next book leans to rest against its neighbor. My book isn't here; I like to think that someone has already checked it out.

Geniza, home library, palace of the people, treasure house, and chicken coop of the muses: my original categories, the Parnassan and the universal, fall away in a maze of overlapping possibilities. Like Borges's Library of Babel, any collection of books contains the seeds of nearly numberless alternatives and contradictions. Although a canon is a constructed thing, the universalizing tendencies that oppose canonization are themselves no less constructed. Ultimately, even the universal library is less a true compendium of the totality of human knowledge—less a model *of* the universe—than simply another kind of ritual representation of collective wisdom. The Library of Congress holds over one hundred million books in 450 languages—a latter-day Babel to be sure, but a mere fraction of the several thousand natural languages and dialects in which people speak and act around the world. With all its fructifying abundance, perhaps the universal library, like the canon-serving Parnassan, is a model *for* as well as a model *of*. Everything exists to end up there.

We see libraries everywhere. Following the intuition of thinkers ranging from Spinoza to Alan Turing, we can conceive of the universe as the shape information takes as it flows and clots, cascades and recombines. Recently, it's been suggested that the universe itself is a computer that stores all data in endless variation; all phenomena, from the scattering of subatomic particles after the Big Bang to the tumbling waves of the Pacific Ocean, to the wingbeats of a monarch butterfly in migratory flight, are computations. Readings.

The bibliographer in the digital age returns to the revelatory practice of her medieval forebears. Librarians, like those scribes of the Middle Ages, do not merely keep and classify texts; they create them, too, in the form of online finding aids, CD-ROM concordances, and other electronic texts, not to mention paper study guides and published bibliographies. Digital texts have followed the same deeply grooved arc of other forms of writing. As in ancient Mesopotamia, where cuneiform writing began as crude hash marks made in wet clay to account for cattle and bushels of grain, the binary texts of the computer age were first inscribed by numerate clerks and economical priests. And yet, in time those hash marks, those graffiti, were stolen by the cults of the muses. Already we call our databases and online catalogs "digital objects"—a reflection, perhaps, of our nostalgia for the dusty physicality of our books (an abundance of which we will continue to curate for some generations to come). Perhaps present-day written texts, translated imme-diately into these evanescent digital media, will be preserved for future generations. But won't those generations be as concerned to preserve the framing data that gloss and illuminate those texts? Won't they search for beauty and truth in the code our programmers mean to make invisible? Almost certainly they will. These digitial texts, these "objects," will be classified, described, and annotated. Undoubtedly, this will be a labor of love. The digital objects of today are the incunabula of a not-too-distant tomorrow—our palimpsests, our geniza bits, the refuse of our restless and inconsolable appetite for change and immortality.

The library in the digital age is in a state of flux, which is indis-tinguishable from a state of crisis—not only for institutions but for the books they contain, preserve, and propagate, a crisis for the cul-ture of letters whose roots are firmly planted in the library. The uni-versal library pretended to answer the question "What belongs in the library?" And yet in a world that seems to make ever more room for information, this question retains its ancient force. Jonathan Swift feared that the inclusion of modern books would ruin the library's canonical force; librarians in more recent, allegedly more liberal times have scrutinized the material in their growing collections with an equally jaundiced eye, presuming to separate wheat from chaff, worthy from worthless. Major libraries everywhere are hemorrhag-ing books by the heap, selling them, pulping them, or storing them in remote warehouses by the millions of volumes. The problems libraries face—lack of space, loss of funding—are real and formida-ble. And the choices they face are Faustian in their many dangers. In his recent book *Double Fold: Libraries and the Assault on Paper*, Nicholson Baker brought indignation to bear on library administra-tors who judged the daily newspaper an ephemeral form unworthy of systematic collection. Its acidic paper they declared too troublesome to store and preserve, its contents too tawdry and quotidian to merit conservation. Yet, ever since John Dunton offered his *Athenian Mercury* as a means of education for the "middling sort" of person, newspapers have been the birthing grounds of the zeitgeist, its writers the often anonymous authors of the public sphere itself. As Baker recounts, newspapers have promoted great leaps in printing technology and have set standards for typographical elegance and graphic beauty that printers of books have long struggled to match. The disappearance of newspapers—their eviction from such allegedly universal collections as those of the British Library, the Library of Congress, the New York Public Library, and countless other libraries—is a loss of historic proportions.

In the ideal public library, we are all readers of the "middling sort." Reading whatever we will, we fulfill a public function, preserving the sacrosanct space of inner thought that is our birthright. Assaults on that birthright in the forms of legislation, surveillance, and censorship ultimately are precisely as dangerous as our acquiescence in them.

What we face is not a loss of books but the loss of a world. As in Alexandria after Aristotle's time, or the universities and monasteries of the early Renaissance, or the cluttered-up research libraries of the nineteenth century, the Word shifts again in its modes, tending more and more to dwell in pixels and bits instead of paper and ink. It seems to disappear thereby, as it must have for the ancient Peripatetics, who considered writing a spectral shibboleth of living speech; or the princely collectors of manuscripts in the Renaissance, who saw the newly recovered world of antiquity endangered by the brute force of the press; or the lovers of handmade books in the early nineteenth century, to whom the penny dreadful represented the final dilution of the power of literature. And yet, the very fact that the library has endured these cycles seems to offer hope. In its custody of books and the words they contain, the library has confronted and tamed technology, the forces of change, and the power of princes time and again.

Such changes are part of that endless cycle of renewal for which the library has its readers to thank. Think of Richard Wright, turning the Jim Crow library that excluded him into an instrument of self-discovery. Think, too, of Walter Benjamin, who for all his distance and difference lived in the very same world that Wright discovered: the forest of books. Benjamin was stopped at a geographical border with an unfinished book in his suitcase. Wright used a borrowed library card like a passport to cross into that same world, where his own books waited for him, unwritten.

Here in the stacks, the library may seem the place where books go when they die. In their totality, they disappear amid their own splendid mystifications. From age to age, libraries grow and change, flourish and disappear, blossom and contract—and yet through them all we're chasing after Alexandria, seeking a respite on Parnassus, haunted by the myths of knowledge and of wholeness that books spawn when massed in their millions. The divine irony that Borges discovered while groping his way through the stacks strikes the sighted librarian just as powerfully: preserving themselves, the books elude us. And yet it's this that inspires more books, goading us to finish them, to complete the set, to add another book to the collection.

Notes on Sources

I have tried to point out most of my sources throughout the text. In what follows, I provide bibliographical information for selected books and authors, especially those that lie outside the scope of general reading. I hope to provide a sense of the trail I followed, and the importance of other authors as guides along the way.

CHAPTER 1: READING THE LIBRARY

Thomas Wolfe's library set piece in his novel *Of Time and the River* (New York: Scribner's, 1935) dramatizes what many students, faculty, and library staff experience in their forays into the Widener stacks. I learned about the life of Giuseppe Arcimboldo in Werner Kriegeskorte's *Giuseppe Arcimboldo* (Cologne: Taschen, 1993). Statistics on book publication around the world I derive from *The Librarian's Companion,*

2nd ed., by Vladimir F. Wertsman (New York: Greenwood Press, 1996), and the *UNESCO Statistical Yearbook* (annual). The Seneca passage is taken from the *Ad Lucilium epistulae morales* of the Loeb Classical Library (Cambridge: Harvard University Press, 1979), with English translation by Richard M. Gummere. Though decidedly old-fashioned, the Loeb series, with its facing Latin text and English translation and its copious notes, remains among the best sources of classical writings for the nonspecialist; unless otherwise noted, I take all subsequent references to classical authors from the Loeb series. Edmund Lester Pearson's essay discussing the challenges of the card catalog is found in *The Library and the Librarian* (Woodstock, Vt.: Elm Tree Press, 1910), a compilation of the author's columns for the *Boston Evening Transcript* and other newspapers. Pearson also wrote *The Old Librarian's Almanack* (Woodstock, Vt.: Elm Tree Press, 1909), one of the most entertaining literary hoaxes of the twentieth century. Pearson's wholly fictional librarian Jared Bean was quoted approvingly by a number of critics, columnists, and librarians. In *Atlas of the European Novel, 1800–1900* (London: Verso, 1998), Franco Moretti sketches the beginnings of a new way of looking at the uses of reading in history, despite an all-too-common prejudice for literary reading as the chief expression of literacy. Stéphane Mallarmé's gnomic biblio-cosmogony is articulated in "As to the Book: The Book, a Spiritual Instrument," which I read in *The Poems: A Bilingual Edition* (New York: Penguin, 1977), translated and edited by Keith Bosley. Mallarmé's great work *Un Coup de dés jamais n'abolira le hasard* (A roll of the dice will never abolish chance) is suffused with the poet's profound ambivalence about the nature and meaning of the book. Henry David Thoreau expresses his own ambivalence in *A Week on the Concord and Merrimack Rivers* (1849). Jorge Luis Borges, of course, was also ambivalent about libraries, in his own rich ways; his story "The Library of Babel" is collected in many places, though I continue to rely on James E. Irby's translation in *Labyrinths: Selected Stories and Other Writings* (New York: New Directions, 1964). I quote Borges's "Poem of the Gifts" from the *Selected Poems* (New York: Penguin, 1999) edited by Alexander Coleman; the translation is Alistair Reid's, and I am grateful for his permission to use it.

CHAPTER 2: BURNING ALEXANDRIA

Alfred J. Butler's *The Arab Conquest of Egypt* (Oxford: Clarendon Press, 1902) is the classic Western Orientalist account of the rise of the caliphate; Mostafa el-Abbadi's *The Life and Fate of the Ancient Library of Alexandria* (Paris: UNESCO, 1992) provides not only a tour of the stories told about the demise of the famous library but also a fresh perspective on post-classical Near Eastern history. My understanding of life in Alexandria's libraries was enriched by several other works as well: *The Library of Alexandria: Centre of Learning in the Ancient World* (London: Tauris, 2000), edited by Roy MacLeod, especially essays by the editor ("Alexandria in History and Myth"), D. T. Potts ("Before Alexandria: Libraries in the Ancient Near East"), Robert Barnes ("Cloistered Bookworms in the Chicken Coop of the Muses: The Ancient Library of Alexandria"), and Samuel N. C. Lieu ("Scholars and Students in the Roman East"). Luciano Canfora evokes the splendor and mystery of ancient Alexandria in his book *The Vanished Library: A Wonder of the Ancient World* (Berkeley: University of California Press, 1990), translated by Martin Ryle. Rudolf Blum's *Kallimachos: The Alexandrian Library and the Origins of Bibliography* (Madison: University of Wisconsin Press, 1991), translated by Hans Wellisch, is a lively scholarly exploration of the meaning of books in the ancient world and the importance of the great lyric poet Callimachus in the history of libraries and the book.

In *The Stele Inscriptions of Chin Shih-huang: Text and Ritual in Early Chinese Imperial Representation* (New Haven: American Oriental Society, 2000), Martin Kern offers lovely translations and nuanced interpretations of the stone inscriptions of the First August Emperor, and discusses their relation to the story of the Qin biblioclasm; his work also introduced me to the very useful word "biblioclasm" (which seems his own coinage). Glen Dudbridge explored the story of the Qin destruction of books in his 1999 Panizzi lectures at the British Library, collected in the volume *Lost Books of Medieval China* (London: British Library, 2000). Burton Watson's translations of Chinese histories are recognized classics, and his edition of Sima Qian's *Annals, Records of the Grand Historian* (New York: Columbia University Press; Hong Kong: Chinese University of Hong Kong, 1993), is no exception. Grant Hardy describes the uses and meanings of reading in early China, and the work and fate of Sima Qian, in his *Worlds of Bronze and Bamboo: Sima Qian's Conquest of History* (New York: Columbia University Press, 1999). *The First Emperor of China* (White Plains, N.Y.: International Arts and Sciences Press, 1975), a collection of essays by scholars of the People's Republic edited by Li Yu-ning, illustrates the political uses to which the story of the Qin biblioclasm has been put. Tsuen-hsuin Tsien's *Written on Bamboo and Silk: The Beginnings of Chinese Books and Inscriptions* (Chicago: University of Chicago Press, 1962) is a highly readable exploration of the history and meaning of writing and books in China; Tsien describes the Fang shan stone library and the importance of stone inscription in the dissemination of Buddhist literature and gives a thorough account of the forms and meanings of the book in China throughout its history. David Diringer's *The Book before Printing: Ancient, Medieval, and Oriental* (New York: Dover, 1982) provides a sound account of the history of the many forms books have taken.

The story of the destruction of the Aztec histories is told in Miguel León-Portilla's groundbreaking work *The Broken Spears: The Aztec Account of the Conquest of Mexico*, translated into English by Lysander Kemp (Boston: Beacon Press, 1992). León-Portilla edited and adapted stories of the conquest of Mexico written by early Nahuatl scribes, which Angela Maria Garibay K. translated into Spanish. I learned more about the forms and meanings of written Nahuatl from

John Bierhorst's *History and Mythology of the Aztecs: The Codex Chimalpopoca* (Tucson: University of Arizona Press, 1992), Gordon Brotherston's *Painted Books from Mexico* (London: British Museum Press, 1995), and Joyce Marcus's *Mesoamerican Writing Systems: Propaganda, Myth, and History in Four Ancient Civilizations* (Princeton: Princeton University Press, 1992).

The eminent classicist Lionel Casson provides a complete picture of the libraries of antiquity in his book *Libraries in the Ancient World* (New Haven:Yale University Press, 2001). His copious and learned classical citations were an invaluable guide to my further reading. Roman libraries are put into context for me most evocatively by the work of Elizabeth Rawson, whose study *Intellectual Life in the Late Roman Republic* (Baltimore: Johns Hopkins University Press, 1985) gives a full picture of the lives and working patterns of Roman intellectuals. I found another perspective on the role of the book in the ancient world in H. L. Pinner's *The World of Books in Classical Antiquity* (Leiden: A.W. Sijthoff, 1948).The story of Herculaneum and its destruction in the eruption of Vesuvius is told in Amedeo Maiuri, *Herculaneum and the Villa of the Papyri* (Novara: Istituto Geografico de Agostini, 1974), and the work of researchers from Brigham Young University and the Italian National Library at Naples is described on the BYU website (www.byu.edu/news/releases/archive01/Mar/Herculaneum/photos.html).

CHAPTER 3: THE HOUSE OF WISDOM

I learned about the possible derivation of the word "book," as well as interesting facts about the use of wax tablets, from R. H. and M. A. Rouse's article, "The Vocabulary of Wax Tablets," *Harvard Library Bulletin*, new series, vol. 1, no. 3 (Fall 1990).The bindings of the books in the Nag Hammadi library are discussed in *The Archaeology of Medieval Bookbinding*, by J. A. Szirmai (Burlington,Vt.: Ashgate, 2000).The story of the Syriac library of Moses of Nisibis, as well as facts about the life of Cassiodorus and the libraries of medieval Islam, I learned from articles by S. K. Padover and Isabella Stone in James Westfall Thompson's *The Medieval Library* (Chicago: University of Chicago Press, 1939). Lisa Jardine discusses the role of books in the lives of illustrious Renaissance men in the book she edited with Anthony Grafton, entitled *From Humanism to the Humanities: Education and the Liberal Arts in Fifteenth- and Sixteenth-Century Europe* (Cambridge: Harvard University Press, 1986); I learned much about Cosimo de' Medici, Niccolò Niccoli, and the San Marco Library from *The Public Library of Renaissance Florence*, by Berthold L. Ullman and Philip A. Stadter (Padua: Antenore, 1972). For Vespasiano, I used the translation by William George and Emily Waters, *The Vespasiano Memoirs: Lives of Illustrious Men of the XVth Century* (Toronto: University of Toronto Press, 1997). I first learned about Vespasiano from my wife's aunt, Flora Greenan; I am thankful to her for the suggestion. Information on the holdings of medieval libraries I gleaned from James Stuart Beddie's *Libraries in the Twelfth Century, Their Catalogues and Contents* (Cambridge: Houghton Mifflin, 1929). Richard and Mary Rouse, cited above, present their research on the contents and uses of the Sorbonne library in their book *Authentic Witness: Approaches to Medieval Texts and Manuscripts* (Notre Dame: University of Notre Dame Press, 1991). L. D. Reynolds and N. G. Wilson's book *Scribes and Scholars: A Guide to the Transmission of Greek and Latin Literature*, 3rd ed. (Oxford: Clarendon Press, 1991), provided further perspectives on the importance of the library in the development of humanism. I rely on the story of the Vatican Library as recounted in *Rome Reborn: The Vatican Library and Renaissance Culture*, edited by Anthony Grafton (Washington, D.C.: Library of Congress, 1993), especially the sections written by Anthony Grafton, James Hankins, and the late Leonard E. Boyle. I also drew upon Vespasiano's *Memoirs* and my own discussions with Massimo Ceresa and other librarians at the Vatican. At the Vatican Library, I consulted the following manuscript sources bearing on the catalogs and circulation procedures of the early Library: Vat.lat.3966 (early circulation records), Vat.lat.3955 (the first catalog), Vat.lat.3967, and Vat.lat.3954 (later catalogs). I read Montaigne's reflections on the library in the *Travel Journal*; the translation is David Frame's (San Francisco: North Point Press, 1983).

CHAPTER 4: THE BATTLE OF THE BOOKS

The history of Harvard's early printed catalogs and the library they indexed is presented in *The Printed Catalogues of the Harvard College Library, 1723–1790*, edited by Hugh Amory and W. H. Bond (Boston: Colonial Society of Massachusetts, 1996). Ilse Vickers explores the importance of Francis Bacon in English thought, as well as the role of the dissenting academies in the educational life of Britain, in *Defoe and the New Sciences* (Cambridge: Cambridge University Press, 1996). *Thomas Hollis of Lincoln's Inn: A Whig and His Books,* by W. H. Bond (Cambridge: Cambridge University Press, 1990), tells the life of this Harvard benefactor who pushed the library, and the college, toward modernity. My view of the early life of Harvard College also depends on the accounts by Bernard Bailyn and Oscar Handlin included in the volume *Glimpses of the Harvard Past*, edited by Bernard Bailyn (Cambridge: Harvard University Press, 1986). The story of the battle of the books is told best in the historian Joseph M. Levine's book *Battle of the Books: History and Literature in the Augustan Age* (Ithaca: Cornell University Press, 1991). For further information, I relied on several editions of published works and collections of letters and printed documents concerning the lives and works of Bentley, Temple, and Wotton that I consulted at the British Library, especially *The Correspondence of Richard Bentley, D.D., Master of Trinity College, Cambridge*, edited by C. Wordsworth (London: J. Murray, 1842), and *A Dissertation upon the Epistles of Phalaris, Themistocles, Socrates, Euripides, and Others, and the Fables of*

Aesop; Wotton's *Reflections upon the Ancient and Modern Learning*; and Temple's *An Essay upon the Ancient and Modern Learning*. The life of John Dunton, fancifully explicated in his own two-volume autobiographical confessions, is more rigorously explored in *The Oracle of the Coffee House*, by Gilbert D. McEwen (San Marino, Calif.: Huntington Library, 1972). Fundamental to my basic understanding of life in London at the end of the seventeenth century is the *Diary of Samuel Pepys*, in the monumental complete edition edited by Robert Latham and William Matthews (Berkeley: University of California Press, 2000). I learned about the history of the Royal Library from Elaine M. Paintin's history, *The King's Library* (London: British Library, 1989). I explored Jonathan Swift's library not only through the Harold Williams book mentioned in the text, *Dean Swift's Library, with a Facsimile of the Original Sale Catalogue and Some Account of Two Manuscript Lists of His Books* (Folcroft, Pa.: Folcroft Press, 1969), but also via William Le Fanu's *Catalogue of Books belonging to Dr Jonathan Swift, Dean of St Patrick's, Dublin, Aug. 19, 1715* (Cambridge: Cambridge University Library, 1988). Forthcoming at this writing is part one of a projected four-volume bibliographic study called *The Library and Reading of Jonathan Swift*, by Heinz J. Vienken and Dirk F. Passmann (Bern and New York: Peter Lang, 2002), which promises a detailed accounting of Swift's use of books, not only those in his own library but also those he consulted elsewhere. Washington Irving's story of the feisty old entombed tome, which appears in his *Sketch Book* (1820), was pointed out to me by my friend and colleague Peter X. Accardo of Houghton Library, whose copy I borrowed for the reading.

CHAPTER 5: BOOKS FOR ALL

I first heard Enoch Soames's story from my friend James Parker (may his own entries in the catalog multiply forever!). The authoritative account of the British Library, which I rely on extensively, is P. R. Harris's *A History of the British Museum Library, 1753–1973* (London: British Library, 1998). I consulted a copy of the first edition of Jacob Abbott's *The Harper Establishment* in Houghton Library; Oak Knoll Books now publishes an easily obtained reprint of the book, which is full of delights. Walter Benjamin's *Arcades Project*, monumental, unfinished, was published in a translation by Howard Eiland and Kevin McLaughlin in 1999 by the Harvard University Press. For Panizzi's story, I drew on two sources: Edward Miller's *Prince of Librarians: The Life and Times of Antonio Panizzi of the British Museum* (London: British Library, 1988), and Panizzi's own *Passages in My Official Life* (printed by C. F. Hodgson [London], 1871). Two books that tell the story of the British Museum catalog from Panizzi's time to the present are Barbara McCrimmon's *Power, Politics, and Print: The Publication of the British Museum Catalogue, 1881–1900* (Hamden, Conn.: Linnet Books, 1981), and A. H. Chaplin's *GK: 150 Years of the General Catalogue of Printed Books in the British Museum* (Aldershot, U.K.: Scolar Press, 1987). In *A New History of the English Public Library: Social and Intellectual Contexts, 1850–1914* (London: Leicester University Press, 1996), Alistair Black gives a powerful account of the British public library movement in turbulent times.

Information on Melville Dewey comes chiefly from the following sources: Wayne Wiegand's *Irrepressible Reformer: A Biography of Melvil Dewey* (Chicago: American Library Association, 1996); *Melvil Dewey: The Man and the Classification*, edited by Gordon Stevenson and Judith Kramer-Greene (Albany: Forest Press, 1983); and Fremont Rider's *Melvil Dewey* (Chicago: American Library Association, 1944). The Harvard librarian William Coswell's partial correspondence is held in the Harvard Archives; I first learned about Coswell's "slip catalogue" from Kenneth E. Carpenter, who also edited and published Emerson's report on the Harvard College Library, in *Harvard Library Bulletin*, vol. 1, no. 1 (Spring 1990). Essays by Adams, Poole, Smith, and Green are found in the first volume of the *American Library Journal* (1876); "Continuity" appeared in the August 30, 1890, issue of *Harper's Weekly*.

CHAPTER 6: KNOWLEDGE ON FIRE

I found the Belgian War Crimes Commission's report on the destruction of the library of the Catholic University of Louvain in a volume of pamphlets (Q 47) in Widener. Valentin Denis's *Catholic University of Louvain, 1425–1958*, translated by Bartholomew Egan, (Louvain: n.p., 1958), charts the history of the university and its library. American interest in rebuilding the library after the First World War is expressed in Theodore Koch, *The University of Louvain and Its Library* (London: J. M. Dent, 1917), where the story of the professor and his buried book also appears; I derive the account of the German drive through Louvain from reports in the *New York Times*, August and September 1914. The history of the Nazi assault on culture is covered admirably by *Nazism, 1919–1945: A Documentary Reader*, edited by J. Noakes and G. Pridham (Exeter: University of Exeter, 1983). I relied on volume 2, *State, Economy, and Society, 1933–1939*, for translations of documents relating to the *Feuersprüche*, Goebbels's involvement in the book burnings of 1933, and the development of Nazi censorship. Margaret F. Stieg's *Public Libraries in Nazi Germany* (Tuscaloosa: University of Alabama Press, 1992) is my source for the story of how the library world responded to the rise of the Third Reich; the University of Alabama Press kindly granted permission to quote Stieg at length. The fate of books in the Shoah is explored in the haunting volume entitled *The Holocaust and the Book: Destruction and Preservation*, edited by Jonathan Rose (Amherst: University of Massachusetts Press, 2001); I am grateful to the University of Massachusetts Press for permission to use material from Zachary M. Baker's translation of Herman Kruk's diary published in that volume; also important to me in this book were Dina Abramowicz's memoir "The Library in the Vilna Ghetto," "The Nazi Attack on 'Un-German' Literature, 1933–1945," by Leonidas E. Hill, "Bloodless Torture: The books of the Roman Ghetto under the Nazi Occupation," by Stanislao G. Pugliese, and András Riedlmayer's "*Con-*

vivencia under Fire: Genocide and Book Burning in Bosnia." András Riedlmayer also provided crucial access to his own notes and archived documentary material relating to the destruction of the Bosnian National and University Library; I am deeply grateful for his guidance. András's remarks about the importance of cultural heritage in ethnic conflict appear in his article "From the Ashes: The Past and Future of Bosnia's Cultural Heritage," in *Islam and Bosnia: Conflict Resolution and Foreign Policy in Multi-ethnic States*, edited by Maya Shatzmiller (Montreal: McGill-Queens University Press, 2002), pp. 98–135. I built my account of the attack on the library from eyewitness statements gathered by András that by the time this book is published will have been entered into the record of The Hague war crimes tribunal. Many of András's witnesses also appear in the documentary film *Burning Books* (2002), directed by Knut Jorfald. I am also grateful to Jeffrey Spurr, Islamic cataloger at Harvard and coordinator of the Bosnia Library Project, for permission to quote his words marking the tenth anniversary of the destruction of the Vijećnica. Of the many books about the Balkan wars of the late twentieth century, the one I found most useful in understanding the role of cultural destruction in Bosnia is Michael A. Sells's *The Bridge Betrayed: Religion and Genocide in Bosnia* (Berkeley: University of California Press, 1996). I am grateful to David Harsent for permission to quote from his versions of the poems of Goran Simic, which are collected in *Sprinting from the Graveyard* (Oxford: Oxford University Press, 1997). I am also grateful to Goran Simic for his encouragement.

Tsering Shakya's *The Dragon in the Land of Snows: A History of Modern Tibet since 1947* (New York: Columbia University Press, 1999) is an impassioned history of Tibet since the Chinese invasion. The state of Tibetan book arts is discussed on the website of the Conservancy for Tibetan Art and Culture at www.tibetanculture.org/culture_traditions/people/language.htm. I also had the opportunity to casually examine a collection of modern Tibetan books newly acquired at Widener

Library. I first learned about the Chiltan Mountain near Quetta, Pakistan, from Karla Bruner's *Sydney Morning Herald* article "Mohammed's Mountain, a Place to Die For" (November 26, 2001). Latif Pedram tells the story of the Taliban's burning of the Hakim Nasser Khosrow Balkhi Cultural Center and other libraries in his article "Afghanistan: The Library Is Burning," at the website of Autodafe, an international organization supporting suppressed writers and artists (www.autodafe.org/autodafe/autodafe_01/art_03.htm).

Eliza Gleason's study *The Southern Negro and the Public Library* (Chicago: University of Chicago Press, 1941) provided crucial data about library service in the Jim Crow era. Elizabeth McHenry writes extensively about African American literary culture in the antebellum period; I read her article " 'Dreaded Eloquence': The Origins and Rise of African-American Literary Societies and Libraries," *Harvard Library Bulletin*, vol. 6, no. 2 (Spring 1996).

CHAPTER 7: LOST IN THE STACKS

David Wachtel, research associate in Special Collections at the Jewish Theological Seminary in New York, first suggested the compelling story of the Cairo geniza to me in a tour of the library. In addition to Schechter's essay (collected in *Studies in Judaism: A Selection* [Cleveland: World, 1958]), I relied on Paul Kahle's description of the geniza documents in his book *The Cairo Geniza* 2nd ed. (Oxford: Blackwell, 1959). Shelomo Dov Goitein's six-volume *A Mediterranean Society: The Jewish Communities of the Arab World as Portrayed in the Documents of the Cairo Geniza* (Los Angeles: Near Eastern Center, University of California, 1967–93), is the most comprehensive and authoritative work on the subject. Toby Lester discusses the early Korans found in the renovation of Yemen's Great Mosque of Sana'a in his article "What is the Koran?" *The Atlantic Monthly* (January 1999). I read Mary Antin's *The Promised*

Land, 2nd ed. (Princeton: Princeton University Press, 1969, first published in 1912), and Alfred Kazin's memoir *New York Jew* (New York: Alfred A. Knopf, 1978). I referenced LC cataloging and subject classifications through the Library of Congress website (www.loc.gov/catdir). The saga of Sanford Berman is well told in documents collected and placed online by Rory Litwin at his terrific Library Juice website (www.libraryjuice.org); the best presentation of Berman's story, as well as his own writings, is in the book *Everything You Always Wanted to Know about Sandy Berman but Were Afraid to Ask,* edited by Chris Dodge and Jan DeSirey (Jefferson, N.C.: McFarland, 1995). You will find this book, as well as many others listed in these notes, in the bibliography section of the library (it will probably have to be a fairly large library, I'm afraid). In LC libraries, they'll be in the Zs; in Dewey libraries, you'll find them in the 010s (bibliographies) and 020 (library science). Other systems abound: in Widener, the Zs are neighbors to the Old Widener bibliography class, the Bs. These two classes of books about books, two stories beneath Harvard Yard in Widener's sepulchral C level, make up the secret arcadia of many a Harvard librarian; their precinct has been my hunting grounds these past few years, and is the true and original source of this book.

Index